T0258140

DINOSAURS
ON-LINE

DINOSAURS
ON-LINE

A GUIDE to the BEST DINOSAUR SITES on the INTERNET

R. L. Jones
and
Kathryn Gabriel

CUMBERLAND HOUSE
NASHVILLE, TENNESSEE

Published by
CUMBERLAND HOUSE PUBLISHING, INC.
431 Harding Industrial Drive
Nashville, Tennessee 37211
www.CumberlandHouse.com

Cover design by Unlikely Suburban Design, Nashville, Tennessee.

Library of Congress Cataloging-in-Publication Data

Jones, R. L., 1948–
    Dinosaurs on-line : [a guide to the best dinosaur sites on the internet] / R. L. Jones and Kathryn Gabriel.
        p. cm.
    Includes index
    ISBN 978-1-63026-315-7
    1. Dinosaurs—Computer network resources—Directories. 2. Internet (Computer network). I. Gabriel, Kathryn. II. Title.
    QE861.35.J66 2000
    025.06'5679—dc21   00-022575

Printed in the United States of America.

2 3 4 5 6 7 8—15 14 13 11 12

For science teachers everywhere
and all who seek the truth
and
To extant friendships

CONTENTS

INTRODUCTION

THERE WERE GIANTS ON the earth in those days. Some were killers with serrated steak knives for teeth and jaws powerful enough to bite off half a ton of meat at a time, while others were one-hundred-ton behemoths who shook the ground as they walked. Some ran in packs wielding razor-sharp scythes, while their would-be victims defended themselves with tanklike armor and spiked horns more than six feet long. These giants had relatives who took to the air with colossal wings or to the seas with mighty flippers. Together they ruled the land, the skies, and the waters for more than 160 million years. And then, with the flash of an exploding meteor, in the dark chill of an endless winter's night, or on a long, weary march into extinction—they vanished.

At least sixty-five million years have passed since the last of the dinosaurs and great reptiles disappeared from the earth in a calamity not yet fully understood. But are they really gone? As strange as it may seem, they are still very much with us. Dinosaur stuff is everywhere nowadays. There are dinosaur documentaries and dinosaur dictionaries, dinosaur theme parks and restaurants, dinosaur dolls and puppets, dinosaur novels and movies. Dinosaurs find their way into television commercials; they show up on billboards, shirts, caps, coffee mugs, and milk bottles. There are even dinosaur cartoon characters and animal crackers. No natural history museum is complete without a few dinosaur fossils. General-interest museums—and occasionally even art museums—ballyhoo them as well. Needless to say, dinosaurs are more popular than ever.

How can this be? How is it possible that these long-dead creatures—gone now for at least sixty-five million years—keep such a powerful hold on the modern mind? It's simple, really. Dinosaurs are fun. They appeal to our imaginations as well as to our scientific curiosity. They fill us with a sense of awe and wonder. They offer insight into the meaning of existence and the proper place of humanity on the wheel of cosmic time.

Since they make learning an adventure, dinosaurs are especially good for students and children. Dinosaur facts and fossils can furnish the raw materials for some really terrific journals and science projects. But more important, a sincere interest in dinosaurs can promote good reading and study habits and spark a lifelong interest in science.

This book is not just for kids and their teachers; it's for dinosaur hobbyists of all ages—the sort of people who might describe themselves as "dino-hunters." It is intended as a companion volume to *Dino Safari,* the popular travel book released in 1999 by Cumberland House Publishing. Something of an illustrated Mesozoic yellow pages, *Dino Safari* guides readers to more than 250 dinosaur museums, parks, and fossil quarries located throughout North America. Now *Dinosaurs On-Line* explains how you can visit those same prehistory attractions and many others as well, via your computer and a link to the World Wide Web.

POINT AND CLICK T. REX

DINO-HUNTING IS an old sport. It dates back to the early nineteenth century when professional geologists and inspired rock hounds on both sides of the Atlantic realized that they were uncovering some very odd remains. These were large fossilized bones— some of them very big indeed—that could not be matched to any known modern animal. Many such mystery fossils were discovered, and anatomists were soon able to reassemble the skeletons of lizardlike giants such as *Megalosaurus* and *Iguanodon.* In 1841, Richard Owen, of the British Museum, electrified the world when he first described these extinct leviathans as "terrible lizards," or, from the Greek—"dinosaurs."

Owen's bold new word appeared in newspapers and journals, firing the vivid imaginations of Victorians who took delight in the notion that fierce reptilian titans once ruled the planet. Unlike many such fanciful ideas, however (it was the Victorian era that gave birth to science fiction), this one would eventually prove at least as much fact as fiction. During the century and a half since Owen coined the term, countless tons of fossils have been unearthed and studied. Hundreds of dinosaur types and species have come to light and their fossilized skeletons reassembled to give us an idea of what these marvelous creatures looked like and how they lived. The footprints they left on muddy Mesozoic floodplains have been analyzed to tell us how fast they ran—or if they ran at all. Even their droppings have been studied to find out what they ate and how they digested it. Paleontologists have made so many extraordinary discoveries and built up such a mass of evidence that no reasonable person could seriously doubt that dinosaurs once reigned as the earth's largest land animals and most formidable predators.

Nearly everything we know today about dinosaurs was learned from fossils, the bones and other solid body parts of long-dead animals turned to stone by natural chemical processes. Fossils are the primary raw material of paleontology. As rare as deposits of useful minerals such as coal, oil, copper, silver, and gold—and in some cases even more valuable—fossils have been prized and sought after by prospectors for nearly two centuries. Wealthy and eccentric nineteenth-century scientists such as O. C. Marsh (1832–99) and E. D. Cope (1840–97) committed their lives and their entire personal fortunes to the search for dinosaur remains. Often the competition between men like Cope and Marsh grew so feverish that it could best be described as all-out war. (Read all about the "Bone Wars" as well as the victories and defeats of Marsh, Cope, and other early dino-hunters in *Dino Safari*.)

Nowadays, dino-hunters are more fortunate. We don't have to fight a war or spend a lifetime or a fortune to learn about dinosaurs. We can do our prospecting on the Internet. Practically everything that has been learned in nearly two centuries of research is posted somewhere on the World Wide Web. All you need is a computer, a link to the Web, a little patience, and a copy of *Dinosaurs On-Line* to show you where to look. Then just point, click, and presto! Say hello to *Tyrannosaurus rex!*

YOUR DINOSAUR FOSSIL TREASURE MAP

IF YOU happen to be interested in dinosaurs, then you owe it to yourself to visit one or more of America's great paleontology collections such as those on display at the National (Smithsonian) Museum of Natural History in Washington, D.C., the American

Museum of Natural History in New York, the Carnegie Museum of Natural History in Pittsburgh, the Field Museum in Chicago, the California Academy of Sciences in San Francisco, or the Royal Tyrrell Museum in the Canadian Province of Alberta. You can learn more in a single afternoon in the halls of these wondrous institutions than by watching a dozen movies the likes of *Jurassic Park*. You'll have loads of fun too. But here's a surprise! You can visit these and other fine museums without ever leaving home.

Most of North America's best natural history museums maintain excellent Web sites complete with virtual tours that allow you to sample the best and most informative displays. And there's much more dinosaur stuff out there on the Internet: professional sites loaded with hard-core scientific data, research institutions offering educational opportunities, fossil quarries, fossils for sale, national parks, paleo-art, and Web pages created by junior paleontologists, just to name a few. It's all right here in *Dinosaurs On-Line:* roaring *T. rexes,* racing *Velociraptors,* soaring pterosaurs, and guides to help you plan your own real-life fossil expeditions.

For your convenience, we've listed more than two hundred of the best dinosaur Web sites. We've included the address of the home page, an in-depth description of what the site has to offer, and a rating to help you decide which sites to visit first. The ratings are indicated by the number of *T. rex* symbols under the address. Those with four *T. rex* symbols are among the best and most fascinating sites we could locate—you can spend all evening enjoying one of these. The three-*T.-rex* and two-*T.-rex* sites are also terrific, and while the single-*T.-rex* sites may not be as colorful, fact-filled, or fast-moving, they are still well worth a visit.

WEB TIPS, CLICK HERE

THE INTERNET is a worldwide group of public and private computers currently linked together by phone lines to exchange information. The computers talk to one another by using common codes, rules, and languages called Internet protocols.

One of the most familiar and fastest growing parts of the Internet is the World Wide Web. The Web is a collection of electronically linked documents that are stored on the Internet. A file you request on the World Wide Web is called a Web page. The pages are made up of text, images, animation, sound, videos, virtual reality, programs, and data. A Web site is a collection of Web pages. A home or index page is your entry point into a Web site.

Getting Connected

ALL YOU need to be part of the Internet and to browse the Web is a computer, a modem, and a phone line. You can establish your own connection to the Internet through an ISP (Internet Service Provider). Or, you might be able to connect to the Internet through a LAN (Local Area Network) provided by your school or job. The ISP pays for a very high-speed connection to the Internet and then offers you access to that connection for a monthly or hourly fee. Most ISPs provide service through a local telephone line. Once you're connected, you can send and receive E-mail and use all the other Internet services for no additional charge. This is your gateway to the Internet. To access the Internet, you use your modem and telephone or cable line to connect to your ISP's computer (the server) and log on to your account.

When the communication link between your computer and the Internet has been established, you open up a "browsing" program like Netscape Navigator or Microsoft Internet Explorer, which sends your requests to the server. The server does all the work while you sit back and view the resulting information in your browser. Although the document you requested might have traveled thousands of miles over high-speed communications lines, the entire process of requesting and receiving a file or sending an E-mail message takes only a few seconds (well, sometimes a few minutes if the page contains a lot of images!).

Browsing the World Wide Web

WHEN YOU want to view a Web page, you open your browsing program and type an URL (Uniform Resource Locator) into the bar at the top of the page. You can recognize Web URL's by their familiar format of www.somecompany.com (seemingly popping up at the bottom of every advertisement and commercial you see). Think of the URL as the address of the page. Make sure you type in the URL *exactly* as it appears, with no spaces or period at the end. If some of the letters in the address are capitalized, then you should capitalize them too.

The ".com" at the end of an address means that the site is owned by a company or private individual using a commercial ISP. Not all Web sites are commercial; some are sponsored by schools, and so their address ends in ".edu." Government sites end in ".gov," and nonprofit organizations end in ".org." In an ad or on television, an URL might be shortened to dinosaurs.com to make it easier, but be sure to type in the whole address anyway, if your browser doesn't do it for you first.

The address for a home page might also look like this: www.some-company.com/~dinosaurs. The "~" tells your browser to go to the first page of that Web site. The "/," or forward slash, is another sign for the index or home page, as in www.somecompany.com/dinosaurs/. All of the other pages will have an ".htm" or ".html" at the end of the URL like this: www.somecompany.com/dinosaurs/t-rex.html. Once you enter the URL and press Return or Enter, your browser retrieves the page, and you're on your way.

When you use the Web, you look at and retrieve Internet information by pointing and clicking on links with your mouse. The mouse controls the movement of the cursor on the screen. When you want to click on something, move the tip of the arrow over it, then click the mouse button—usually the left button.

The most important thing to remember about the Web is that it is mostly a series of links; some links lead to other pages, some lead to other parts of the same page (and some lead to different Web sites). Spotting the links on a page is essential for surfing the Web. Try clicking on lots of different places in the window to find links. Links are usually represented by:

- Underlined text, usually in a different color from that of surrounding text
- Pictures of any sort, especially:
  —pictures of buttons that say "Home," "Next," "Back," or "E-Mail"
  —pictures that are in a box
  —pictures that look 3-D

—pictures that look as if they lead somewhere (for example, a house usually leads to a home page, and an envelope or mailbox leads to the window where you can send a message to the Web master, or the person who created the Web page)

To go back a page, click on the Back button in your browser, or on a button within the Web page, which will have a left-pointing arrow, the word *Back*, or both.

If there's a page you really enjoy or one that contains a lot of valuable information you may need later, make sure you find out how to save the URL in your browser by "bookmarking" it or adding it to "Favorites." While it's great fun to zoom from page to page or site to site, you also need a way to get back to pages you've already seen or favorite pages from a few sessions ago.

Searching for Information

IF YOU'VE ever looked around on the Web, you know that the information available is—for all practical purposes—endless. The task of trying to find a particular item or piece of information on the Web can also be endless. To speed things up, use indexes and search engines to help you find the information you are seeking. Search engines let you browse by categories, such as sports, arts, entertainment, travel—and dinosaurs.

Search engines work by looking for your specified word or phrase in the millions of Web pages that they know about. After completing the search, the engines display a listing of links to the pages on the Web that may include the text you want. These results are often presented in order of relevance, that is, how likely it is you'll find what you're looking for. Some of the better known search engines are Excite (www.excite.com), Yahoo! (www.yahoo.com), Webcrawler, Google, InfoSeek, and Alta Vista. Search engines will offer tips on refining your search so that you aren't swamped with thousands of unwanted results.

Sometimes a search can turn up dozens or even hundreds of pages, and the pages you want will not always be at the top of the list. Try the first ten or so Web sites, and you may find what you are after. The best sites offer a list of links to recommended Web sites. Most of these lists include other links to worthy sites with material related to the subject, so you probably could surf from one site to another indefinitely. Many times, unfortunately, the links are "broken," meaning they weren't typed in correctly, or are "dead," meaning the Web site is no longer in service or that it has a new address.

Enjoying the Multimedia Experience

WEB PAGES are becoming more interesting, exciting, and interactive every day. Every month new tools appear. Pages are quickly moving from boring fields of tiny text on backgrounds that look like couch fabric, to full color, high-quality, multimedia extravaganzas. The images, sounds, animations, videos, and virtual reality worlds contained in a Web page are not part of the actual page itself, but are separate files sent with the pages in which they appear. When a server sends a Web page and its associated files to your computer, your browser receives and loads the HTML file first, and then loads the graphics and other multimedia files. The HTML file controls the layout of the page, including the placement of all the separate elements.

Graphics files in a Web page come in one of two types: GIF (Graphics Interchange Format) files or JPG (Joint Photographic Expert Group) files. You don't need additional software to view most graphics; however, the files can take a long time to download depending on their size.

To view or hear other multimedia components in a Web page, you often need a "plug-in" or "helper application." A plug-in is a small file stored within a special folder that extends the capabilities of your browser. Plug-ins are distributed by the companies that make the graphics, sound, video, animation, or virtual reality software. While viewing some of the pages described in *Dinosaurs On-Line,* you may need plug-ins like QuickTime, RealPlayer, and Macromedia Shockwave. Usually the Web site using the plug-in will give you a link to the company for the free plug-in download. It can take anywhere from ten minutes to an hour and a half to download the plug-in or the upgrade required. It is almost always worth the time it takes to do this.

Keep in mind that the Web browsers themselves are also being updated constantly, and it might be worthwhile to download the latest version of Microsoft's Internet Explorer or Netscape Navigator. You can do this from within your own browser, usually for free or at a low cost. America Online users will receive upgrades automatically, as will users of some of the other national companies like Earthlink, etc. If you are a user of AOL, know that you are not obligated to use that browser. Some graphics look better in Netscape. Simply connect to AOL, minimize the window, and open Netscape to view the pages you want to see.

Patience Is a Virtue on the Web

PATIENCE IS certainly needed when surfing the Web. Pages with large pictures or a lot of content are sometimes slow to load, and often the Internet itself is just slow. Also, when things seem to be so slow that you suspect they've stopped, your network connection may have gone down (perhaps your phone is disconnected, your Internet software needs to be restarted, or your Internet service provider is down). Try to avoid a lot of clicking ahead; clicking over and over on a spot won't make the page load any faster and will probably slow things down. If you click on a link before a page has finished loading, you will interrupt the transfer of data, so it is a good idea to click the stop sign on your browser before going to the next page. Sometimes links going to later places within that page won't all work, and the computer won't tell you why. At this point, reload the page. To do this, click on the Reload or Refresh button.

Some pages no longer exist. When this is the case, you'll usually get a message telling you that the file was not found. At this point, going back to the previous page (using the Back button) is the easiest option. Sometimes the ISP might just be down. An error message will say "DNS not found." Try the URL again at another time. If any link in this book comes up "Page Not Found," try typing in the address for just the home page. (For example, the home page for www.somecompany.com/dinos/extinction.html would be www.somecompany.com/dinos/.) You can also search for the site by its title or author in a search engine. The site may have changed servers.

A Word About Safety

ALL OF the Web sites recommended in this book have been thoroughly reviewed for content. While none portray bad language or promote dangerous behavior, we can't guarantee that some won't add this in the future.

Sometimes you may want to send an E-mail message to the owner of the Web page, sign up for a newsletter or new information, or leave a message on a bulletin board. If this is the case, make sure that you only give your first name or screen name and *never* give out any personal information about yourself that might put you in danger. If you are a minor (under eighteen years of age) and must include your last name for a newsletter subscription, ask a parent or guardian to do this for you using his or her first and last names.

CHAPTER 1

DINO FUN

BBC Online—Walking with Dinosaurs
www.bbc.co.uk/dinosaurs/index.shtml

Walking with Dinosaurs is designed to promote and supplement a television series by the same name that aired in the fall of 1999 on Great Britain's BBC Television. On the surface this is a nicely designed and easy-to-follow site, with cute graphics that light up when your cursor crosses over them, and informative articles about dinosaurs in the United Kingdom. Dig deeper, and you'll discover an incredible array of interactive movies with computer-animated dinosaurs that look so real you'll think they're alive. This site is not equaled anywhere on the WWW!

Fact Files is not your ordinary, tiresome list of dinosaurs. The title does not do justice to this invaluable resource, not to mention the time, money, talent, and expertise that went into the making of it. On the *Fact Files* index page, you can search for dinosaurs by time, behavior, or diet. A form gives you choices to tick off: For instance, choosing the Late Triassic Period, walking, and carnivore yielded the two dinosaurs—the *Coelophysis* and *Postosuchus*—who lived 215 to 222 million years ago. Click on their images for a pop-up screen that not only displays dino stats and descriptions, but also an animated 3-D graphic, as well as a video clip of the dinosaur, complete with sound effects. QuickTime is needed for the animation, and RealPlayer is needed for the movie (it is well worth the time it takes to download these players). You can send this image or the whole page to a friend as a post card. Alternatively, you can search through the alphabetical glossary, *A to Z*, for the dinosaur of your choice, or click on dino pictures on a *Family Tree* chart. Those names that are in boldface and underlined lead to more animation and movies.

The real gem on this site is *Dinosaur Worlds,* offering six interactive movies, each based on the theme of a television episode. Macromedia Shockwave is essential to play the Flash movies, but it only takes ten to fifteen minutes to download. Additionally, each program must be downloaded, which also takes between ten and fifteen minutes. (We recommend using a program like Netscape's SmartDownload or NetZip, which can download more than one file at a time. Go to home.netscape.com/computing/download/index.html and click on *SmartDownload.*)

Each interactive episode of Walking with Dinosaurs is a cluster of movie clips that play as you select hidden trigger points or action links on the screen in each scene. "New Blood," the series premiere, is about the Late Triassic Period. In the interactive movie, you will catch a fish with a *Coelophysis* and struggle through the dry season. Would a scorpion make a tasty meal? Discover the world of the *Diplodocus* and watch an egg hatch in "Time of the Titans," about the Late Jurassic Period. A *Diplodocus* encounters the fearsome spiked tail of a *Stegosaurus. Liopleurodon* rules the waves in "A Cruel Sea." Can an *Ophthalmosaurus* give birth before it arrives? In "Beneath a Giant's Wing," you get a pterosaur's-eye view of the world and undertake an epic journey back to the mating ground of the *Ornithocheirus.* A *Leaellynasaura* braves the polar winter and tries to stay out of the way of a hungry dwarf allosaurus in "Spirits of the Silent Forest." In "Death of a Dynasty," guard a *Tyrannosaurus* nest from predators and encounter an angry *Ankylosaurus* before the end of the dinosaurs' world. When you click on the program title from within the Web page, provided you have already downloaded it, it still takes another few minutes for the program to open.

Under *Games and Quizzes* you'll find more reasons to have current versions of Shockwave and RealPlayer. Click on *Web Cam* to watch the *Coelophysis* at feeding time. On *Timeline,* the extinction game, you'll try to catch one of the many dinosaurs zooming by with your cursor and drag it to the period in which it lived. If you get it right, the creature will disappear. By the end of the game, all of the creatures will be extinct. There are screensavers, competitions, and mix-and-match games on this page. Viewers, particularly children, can send in their favorite dino tales or drawings for possible publication on the Web site.

This is an incredible site—we can't say it enough—with very few glitches in the fast-loading technology. Be prepared to spend some time here. (And we can't wait until *Walking with the Dinosaurs* comes to PBS!)

Dann's Dinosaur Reconstruction
American Site:
www.geocities.com/CapeCanaveral/4459/
Australian Mirror Site:
home.alphalink.com.au/~dannj/

Dann's Dinosaur Reconstructions is all about Australian dinosaurs. The index page begins with a list of fourteen specific Australian dinosaur reconstructions. One such reconstruction is of a neoceratopsian (pronounced nee-oh-sair-ah-tops-ee-ann), meaning "new horned face."

In 1994 a fossil ulna (lower arm bone) was found in Early Cretaceous (Aptian) deposits in Victoria, Australia. The fossil bore a striking resemblance to the ulna of *Leptoceratops gracilis* from the Late Cretaceous (Maastrichtian) of Canada. The bone itself is about sixteen centimeters long and is missing its funny bone (the olecranon process). Like all ceratopsian ulnae it is short and deep and flat—no other dinosaur has a forearm like this. The New Horned Face featured on Dann's site was reconstructed based on the *Leptoceratops gracilis*. The problem is that the first neoceratopsian, the *Protoceratops andrewsi* from Mongolia, first appears in the fossil record about thirty million years after the one found in Australia. The Canadian specimen appears fifty million years after the Australian specimen. If the Australian fossil is accepted as ceratopsian, then it would place the origins of the neoceratopsian much earlier than was once thought, and on the opposite side of the planet.

Dann's Dinosaur Reconstructions includes a map of each find, charts, artistic renderings of the dinosaur reconstructions, and photographs or drawings of the fossils. Click on the map, or scroll to the bottom of the index page and click on *Australian Dinosaur Sites* for descriptions of the places where the dinosaur fossils and bones were found.

Dann's also provides a link to *Dinosaur Trackways*, boasting that Australia has some of the best, if not *the* best, tracks in the world, in contrast to its meager dinosaur skeletal remains. Dann's divides the trackway descriptions into those found in Queensland (Lark Quarry) and Victoria, and old and new sites in western Australia. Other links include *More Australian Dinosaurs*, Australian fossils, marine reptiles, pterosaurs, hypsilophodontids, polar dinosaurs, references, and reviews of Australian dinosaur books (a couple of which may have been written by the Web author himself).

This site is scientifically based and well organized, while also being on the bright, colorful side with a green dinosaur background scene that looks like drapery. Some of the text is white on a dark background, and while pleasing to the eyes, it will not print out. Don't forget to click on the large red title, *Dann's Dinosaur Reconstructions,* to hear the roar of the dinosaurs.

The Geocities mirror site is more than a simple reflection of the Australian site. It links to *Velociraptor* fossils and a picture gallery that shows thumbnails of all the images used in the site, plus a page of dinosaur cursors and software, as well as an animated dino that demonstrates not only how fast it ran, but also how long it takes to download. The Dinosaur Encyclopedia software advertised on the site looks worthwhile. It includes detailed information on more than 370 valid genera: size, era, location, references, fossils, and species, with location maps for each. It contains more than 250 illustrations and a forty-thousand-word essay section on the usual controversies thoroughly covered in most dinosaur Web sites, which will be described in reviews throughout this book.

Dinogeorge's Home Page
hometown.aol.com/dinogeorge/index.html

George Olshevsky is an inveterate writer on the subject of dinosaurs, with a number of magazine and E-zine (electronic magazine) credits, and is widely referred to in many sites on the Web. It occurred to us that people might like to see his Web site. Of use is The Dinosaur Genera List, an "alphabetized list comprising all dinosaur generic names known to have been published anywhere, with or without formal scientific descriptions." He talks about his dinosaur works-in-progress, such as *The Dinosaur Folios,* an illustrated, encyclopedic treatment of the dinosaurs—all the dinosaurs—in loose-leaf format: everything he has in his files about every species.

Amusing to us was the pitch for the sale of his Jonas Brothers/ Sinclair *Apatosaurus* machette: a one-tenth scale model of the life-size 1964 New York World's Fair Sinclair Pavilion *Apatosaurus,* mounted on a plaque. It's about seven feet long and two feet tall. It "has the wrong head (of course). It is the biggest of the dinosaurs Jonas Brothers worked on (naturally). Shipping and crating will be a problem: the model weighs a good 50 lbs., probably more, and needs careful handling. If you want it, consider driving a van to San Diego to pick it up in person."

All in all, this is a hodgepodge of notes and links crammed into a single Web page.

Dino Hunt
www.sjgames.com/dinohunt/

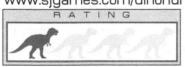

Dino Hunt is a family game for two or more players, ages eight and up. In Dino Hunt, you travel through different eras where the dinosaurs lived to capture them for your modern-day zoo. But the other players have cards that can make your hunt harder—and watch out for that charging *T. rex!* Simple to learn and easy to play, Dino Hunt carries the Dinosaur Society Seal of Approval, because all dinosaur information and art in the game conforms to current scientific knowledge.

Dino Hunt (a game you can purchase through this site) features more than a hundred different dinosaurs. Each oversize card has full-color art from some of the best dinosaur artists in the world. The back of each card gives the most up-to-the-minute scientific data the experts can provide. The basic Dino Hunt package includes 119 cards, full-color rules, and four plastic dinosaurs for playing pieces. "Booster packs" of Dino Hunt cards include all the cards from the boxed set, plus 121 new ones. The booster cards are gold-bordered and dated 1996 to distinguish them from the cards in the basic game. These gold-bordered cards will not be reprinted—this is a true limited edition. And every POP set contains at least one gold foil "fossil" Ultra-Rare card.

The Dino Hunt site contains links to the latest news on Dino Hunt and dinosaur discoveries, tournament rules, educational use of Dino Hunt, a curriculum guide for parents and teachers, a *Dino Hunt Scientific Update and Errata, The Dino Hunt Art Gallery,* what people are saying about Dino Hunt, and other cool dinosaur links. Players are invited to submit ideas for new Dino Hunt cards.

Cool game, but boring Web site.

DinoMorph Project
www.cs.uoregon.edu/~kent/dinoMorph.html

A thirty-ton *Apatosaurus* was something of a huge Jurassic cow, head just above the ground, well placed to graze on ferns and horsetails (no grass back then, remember). How do we reconstruct its pose and flexibility? While the original specimen is mounted in a steel framework, as is the exquisite specimen CM 3018 on the floor of the Carnegie Museum of Natural History, the essential dimensions have been replicated in a 3-D model by a computer program named DinoMorph.

DinoMorph is a software being developed for vertebrate pale-ontologists, educators, and anyone else interested in studying skel-etal structures. The "Dino" in the name means that the software is being driven by research in dinosaur paleontology. The "Morph" signifies one of its major abilities: morphing (continuously inter-polating) between two taxa, or morphing between two poses; it also signifies morphology and morphometrics, the field of quanti-fying and comparing shape.

The DinoMorph project began in 1994 as a software engineer-ing exercise in an undergraduate course at the University of Oregon Department of Computer and Information Science. With encour-agement by paleontologists such as Dr. James Kirkland and Dr. Michael Parrish, DinoMorph became a useful research tool for examining skeletal biomechanics. They showed Kent Stevens (the Web site author), while standing beneath a sauropod skeleton in Vernal, Utah, that very little is really known about how sauropod dinosaurs moved, how they posed themselves, and why they devel-oped their extraordinary specializations. The necks were particu-larly intriguing, being so long and obviously specialized in function. But for what function? Clearly, some of the design reflected sculpt-ing to reduce weight and to direct compressive loads. But function-ally, as articulated, jointed systems, how did they work, and how far could they bend the neck? How far could they permit the dinosaur to reach up to feed, or bend around to look about?

DinoMorph's genesis is explained in this Web site, illus-trated by computer images of the *Apatosaurus* posed at different angles. Three of these images can be viewed in their animated sequence on *National Geographic*'s dinorama, "Moving Mon-sters" (www.nationalgeographic.com/dinorama/sauro.html). You can also find some DinoMorph images in Carl Zimmer's cover story in the November 1997 issue of *Discover* magazine (the text of which is archived at *Dinosaurs in Motion*). Stay tuned to DinoMorph for a gallery of previously unpublished images. Read more about Kent Stevens and his work on his home page at www.cs.uoregon.edu/~kent/index.html#paleo.

Dino Paradise
www.vcnet.toyama.toyama.jp/~saurs/sc_index.htm

The author of this site calls himself "Hypersaurs"—that's not his real name, of course. A pharmacist by trade, Hypersaurs says he loves dinosaurs and created this Web site because no other English sites existed about Japanese dinosaurs. Here you will find intriguing bits of information about Japanese museum exhibits and dinosaur finds, such as a theropod tooth, fossilized eggshell fragments, a *Toyama-sauripus masuiae* footprint, and photos of two *Sinosauropteryx* fossils, one with a lizard in its gut, and the other with tiny eggs inside it. These can be viewed by following the *Gallery* link. Pay special attention to *Mineral Fair '97* for photos of *Confuciusornis*, which he says was "cute." See *Dino Tour* for a few notes on a trip to Korea to view Mongolian trackways. *Dino Museum* is a cybermuseum that Hypersaurs created to pass on news of Japanese dinosaurs and to tell about Japanese dinosaur books. Judging from the odd computer characters, a lot was lost in the translation from Japanese to English.

Dino Russ's Lair
www.isgs.uiuc.edu/dinos/

Are you interested in participating in a real dinosaur dig? Do you want to learn more about the discovery of new specimens? Do you want to share in the thrill of the discovery of fossil treasures? Are you interested in the techniques employed by vertebrate paleontologists to remove dinosaurs and other vertebrate fossils from the field? Do you like outdoor work? Do you like strenuous conditions as well as painstaking and tedious work?

If you answered yes to these questions, then here is your chance to participate in a real dino-dig. At Dino Russ's Lair, you will find information on how you can join a dig, including one that might involve Dino Russ himself.

Dino Russ Jacobson is associate geologist at Illinois State Geological Survey with vast experience as a paleontologist and computer programmer. His lair might not be the den or dwelling of a wild animal, but it is certainly one place to go for all kinds of links to dinosaur information (in general and specifically in Illinois), art, digs, exhibits, eggs, tracks, sites, societies, and publications. This is no ordinary Web director—Russ (and his Web master) include descriptions of each link. More important, all of his links are updated regularly. Of particular interest to Russ are paleontological digs around the country. He provides detailed information about different digs and links to companies sponsoring digs.

The best dinosaur directory on the World Wide Web!

Dinosauria On-Line
www.dinosauria.com/
Mirrored on Dino Russ's Lair
www.isgs.uiuc.edu/dinos/index2.html

If all roads led to Rome, all Web sites about dinosaurs link to Dinosauria On-Line (DOL). This is undoubtedly one of the best and most thorough dinosaur home pages on the World Wide Web. It has all the ingredients for a real Web adventure: a clever safari design, lots of information, great graphics, a search engine, site map, clear traffic signs for easy navigation, plus remote-control navigation (the navigation bar floats over every page when selected), and it even downloads quickly. You can find almost anything you might want to know about the latest discoveries and thinking here on these pages, and it is all clearly and crisply written, mostly by Jeff Poling himself. Be sure to click on *Full Index Page* to see the table of contents.

Just so you know, Jeff says: "Dinosaurs were warm-blooded, *T. rex* was a fearsome predator, and birds ARE dinosaurs . . . because it just wouldn't be cool any other way." Jeff may be opinionated, but he is also scientifically oriented, and he says the fossil evidence shows these things to be true. In fact, he created DOL to give the Web reader broader exposure to dinosaur science, and to talk about the topics that are hot among dinosaur enthusiasts today. This allows readers to not only see a subject from many points of view but also to see what others think about ideas and questions readers often are unable to pose to knowledgeable people.

Dinosauria On-Line is meant for the serious enthusiast and rank amateur alike. Discussions are technical, but you don't need a Ph.D. to understand and enjoy them. Original articles written specifically for DOL are intended to clear up certain issues (such as the meaning of terms like "warm-blooded") for dinosaur new-comers, and to clarify meanings for those already deeply enmeshed in the subject. Dictionaries, maps, and lists also help define important terms and clarify the technical information presented both here and in publications. Pictures are used where possible to clarify or emphasize important points.

The real gem of the site is the *Journal of Dinosaur Paleontology*. Read articles and discussions from enthusiasts and actual paleontol-ogists on various dinosaur topics. For instance, one article is about the discovery of the fossil remains of the holy Confucius bird (*Confuciusornis sanctus*). Did you know that this was the earliest bird known to have replaced the toothy jaws of its reptilian ancestors with an avian-style beak?

All fossil hunters should be aware of the laws regarding fossils. An important chunk of the journal is the invaluable and lengthy section on legal issues. Here you can read the laws for yourself.

The *Dinosaur Omnipedia* is a tremendous feat in and of itself. It offers anatomica-l and paleontological-terms dictionaries, a transla-tion and pronunciation guide, lists of dinosaur genera, cladograms, the names and dates of all the geological time periods, and maps of ancient earth. There's even a writer's guide to show how to use dino-saur names in a sentence.

The site's *Dino Dispatches* pulls together information from vari-ous sources that provide up-to-date reviews of new discoveries and new thinking on topics related to dinosaurs and other Mesozoic ani-mals. If all this weren't enough, DOL also showcases dinosaur art by various well-known artists in the *Gallery*. Be sure to stop by the *DinoStore* for fine fossil replicas by Skullduggery.

Jeff Poling graduated from Ohio State University with a bachelor of science in aeronautical and astronautical engineering "two days before the aerospace industry collapsed," and returned to school for more degrees in business and computer science. He says his childhood interest in dinosaurs was reawakened by the movie *Jurassic Park*. Soon after, he began devouring dinosaur books, beginning with *Bakker's Dinosaur Heresies, Horner's Digging Dinosaurs,* and *The Complete T Rex*. "As my knowledge of the subject grew I found myself wanting to discuss my knowledge and ask questions that were plaguing me, but had nowhere to turn. At this time I became active on the Internet. I scoured the Web for dinosaur information, but never found what I was really looking for. Hence the genesis of Dinosauria On-Line."

Dinosauria On-Line is a very popular Web site. It receives three to five times the traffic of the nearest commercial Web account and as much as 110,000 times the traffic of others. Jeff accepts donations to offset the commercial rates his provider has threatened to charge.

Dinosaur Illustrated Magazine
illustrissimus.virtualave.net/dimfront.html
Beri's Dinosaur World
www.geocities.com/CapeCanaveral/Lab/1638/index.html
See also: Illustrissimus Central Home Page
illustrissimus.virtualave.net/index.html

Dinosaur Illustrated magazine (*DIM*) covers the latest discoveries in the field of vertebrate paleontology. This Web magazine is devoted to the art and science of restoring and reconstructing dinosaurs and other extinct higher tetrapods, and is really designed to display artwork presented by the international illustrator and editor Berislav Krzic (Illustrissimus Productions).

Many of the illustrated articles that have been posted since November 1998 are still available to the public. "Feathers, Feathers Everywhere," for example, introduces the new Chinese dinosaur sensation: a feathered therizinosaur, which ruffled the feathers of the vertebrate paleontology community. In March 1999, Beri brought in Steve Brusatte (see Dino Land Web site in chapter 4) on an article called "A New Mosasaur Discovered," as the first of a long line of guest authors. Others include Brian Fraczak's "Colossal Cretaceous Crocs," Jack Conrad's "The Problematic Therizinosauroids: The nature of the beasts," and James Farlow's "A Night on Par Pond." Other articles are available by subscription only. These include: "A Mesozoic Parrot? A Mesozoic Parrot!," "The New Giant German Theropod," and "The Second Italian Dinosaur." Subscription is free.

Beri's Dinosaur World (*BDW*) is another showcase of extinct animals drawn by Berislav Krzic and is more a collection of art with lots of notes about how to sketch and reconstruct dinosaurs. Particularly amusing are the tongue-in-cheek Dino Safari Photos, such as the one of a *Utahraptor* caught in a brushfire, taken on March 6, 124,241,998 B.C., or the small ornithopod under a tree he photographed while walking near the beach in Istria (Croatia) on March 5, 91,071,998 B.C.

Enjoy the ride into the past, Beri says. "See the animals that once roamed the earth, mighty and beautiful, but now gone. We only have a *DIM* glimpse at the ancient world, but we're trying hard to see it better and more each and every day."

These sights are visually appealing and well organized. Despite the warning to be patient while graphics download, the site is quick.

Dinosaur Interplanetary Gazette
Frontpage-All the Dinosaur News that's Fit to Print
www.dinosaur.org/

Dinosaur Interplanetary Gazette (*DIG*) is a monthly electronic magazine, and like all glossy magazines in print, large color ads cover a large chunk of the publication. That's how they make their money to continue publishing. *DIG* has more than twenty awards to prove its entertaining and educational value. The interactive quality alone, such as the message-board dialogue with famous paleontologists, is probably what keeps them coming back for more. But waiting for the large files to download and then wading through the blinking and twirling animation and miles of book reviews (the reason for the slow download time), might wear thin for those who just want the facts, ma'am. It is difficult to see the forest for the trees, or, in this case, the dinosaurs for the ads.

As *DIG* warns, the *Frontpage* (the main page of the site) is indeed "the world's longest and most ridiculous." After spending a day or two exploring this page, we discovered a button buried deep on the side for a window that displays a Dino Guide to the site. We learned the hard way that clicking on the *Frontpage* link from outside the page causes it to completely reload—and that isn't necessary when you've already got it cached on your hard drive. The best way to return to the *Frontpage* is to use your browser's Back button or History menu. Sometimes there is so much traffic that a message comes up from the server telling you the page is now busy and to come back in an hour. (If this happens, we found that you can still use the Back button to get to the *Frontpage*.) But the Dino Guide window is always open and is the best mode of navigation. Another way to get a handle on the site is the *Saur-o-Find-o-Matic,* a site map that opens up as a separate window. You'll find an experimental search at the top of this page in fine print. At the bottom of the *Saur-o-Find-o-Matic* are links to advertising rates and information about the editorial staff.

The "Personal Appearance Department" is where you click on *Dinosaur Interplanetary Gazette Dino Dish* to go to the message board, where many hours of your life can be sucked up as you follow all of the message threads. Paleontologists are regularly brought on as guests here, and readers are invited to fill out an E-mail form at the bottom of the page to participate in the conversation chain. When we checked out the site, Drs. Philip Currie and Eva Koppelhus, from the Royal Tyrrell Museum of Canada, were at the helm.

Along this same line, Dr. Fred Bortz, not a paleontologist but an author of dino books, writes a regular column based on questions from the audience (you). If a question is used in *Ask Dr.*

Fred, a student will receive a free book, and his or her school will receive one hundred dollars off the price of a personal appearance by Dr. Fred.

Famous and not-so-famous "dinosaur detectives," such as museum curators, writers, and paleontologists, are interviewed in the *Bone Zone.* A few examples include Michael K. Brett-Surman of the Smithsonian, Kenneth Carpenter of the Denver Museum, and author James O. Farlow. *Dinosaur Time Machine* features articles on historical figures who ushered in the young field of paleontology.

Click on the *Dino News Network* to taste satisfying "Dino Bites" and "News Nibbles," ranging from new discoveries to voting for postage stamp dinosaurs. *Dino Feature Stories* links to short pieces that might remotely have to do with dinosaurs, such as "Dinosaurs on Broadway (Well, almost)," about a dinosaur costume appearance in a play; "Filming Ancient Sharks," for *Paleoworld* on the Learning Channel; "Dragons, Dinosaurs and China," about the connection between dragons and dinosaurs; and "Einstein Tells a Joke."

Dino Calendar is a worthwhile feature where readers can find information about conferences, digs, symposiums, and exhibits around the world. Job opportunities are promised for future posting. Another nice feature is the *Geologic Timeline* that pops up as a separate window. Bookmark this page for future school reports (www.dinosaurs.org/timeline.htm). *Dinosaur Reports for School and Research Type Stuff* walks students through the process of writing a report, offering resource links and a search engine (www.dinosaur.org/schoolreport.htmll).

The rest of the links go to reviews of books, movies, and music about dinosaurs.

Dinosaurs!
www.geocities.com/CapeCanaveral/Hall/2830/index.html

As the introduction states, Dinosaurs! intends to offer a little information about dinosaurs and is designed for people of all ages who have a general interest in the marvelous creatures. Here you will find descriptions of the Triassic, Jurassic, and Cretaceous Periods, diagrams, time lines, charts, and several images and descriptions of some of the Web author's favorite dinosaurs. As an added bonus, students who need help with school projects are invited to E-mail the author for assistance. (Please refer to the section "A Word About Safety" in the introduction.)

Besides a general overview of the "terrible lizards," the site offers *Dino FAQs* (Frequently Asked Questions). No question is too foolish. For instance: "Did humans have dinosaurs for pets like Fred Flinstone's Dino?" Fair enough. Answer: "Contrary to the fantasy world of Fred Flinstone, humans and dinosaurs did not live on this earth at the same time. The first humans did not arrive on the scene until dinosaurs had been extinct for about 63 million years. However, it's always fun to imagine what a dinosaur pet would be like! (As long as it wasn't a T-Rex!)"

Other brief topics include the great debate over whether birds are descendants of dinosaurs, and whether dinosaurs were warm-blooded or cold-blooded. This page talks about the discovery of *Archaeopteryx* (Ancient Bird). The author also discusses the extinction theories. The most valuable piece on this site is the discussion of paleontology as a career. (So you want to be the next Robert Bakker?) This page defines the job of a paleontologist and some of the specialties within the field. It also lays out a study course for preparing to be a paleontologist and also provides a list of good universities in the United States and Canada for paleontology.

This site is beautifully and expertly designed and organized in a frames format, which, in this case, is helpful and discreet.

Dinosaurs Dinosaurs Dinosaurs!
Dino Don Lessem
www.dinodon.com/index.html

"Dino" Don Lessem is a world-renowned dinosaur expert and writer. He has written on dinosaurs and other scientific subjects for numerous newspapers and magazines, including the *Boston Globe*, the *New York Times*, the *Smithsonian*, and *Omni*. He is the author or coauthor of many books on dinosaurs, including: *Bigger Than T. rex*, *Dinosaurs Rediscovered*, and, with Dr. John R. Horner, *The Complete T. Rex* and *Digging Up Tyrannosaurus Rex*. He hosted and wrote NOVA documentaries and is the creator and host of the largest and most successful traveling dinosaur exhibit in North America: "The Dinosaurs of Jurassic Park/The Lost World." Don also produces the Giganotosaurus.com Web site, devoted to information and news about the largest carnivorous dinosaur ever found (www.dinodon.com/gig_index.html)..

Navigating the site is like turning the pages of a children's book, with the bright reds and yellows and the clever dinosaur animation that marks each page. Kids are invited to send in their dinosaur drawings and paintings for possible publication on Dino Don's pages. They can view the work of the world's foremost dinosaur artists in the *Dinosaur Art Gallery*, which features a changing parade of artists. Every month, children can meet a new paleontologist who will answer E-mail questions. They can read about some of Dino Don's latest adventures in *Dino News*. In April 1999, for instance, he went to Patagonia, Argentina, where paleonotologists were excavating five giganotosaurs.

Children have an opportunity to buy books by Don Lessem or casts and sculptures of giganotosaur teeth and skulls from *Cool Dinosaur Stuff*. Children can also read an ongoing fictional saga about a *Troodon* named Dorla, who must make her way past a pack of carnivores to lay her eggs in duckbill nests. Duckbills will raise *Troodon* hatchlings as their own until they are old enough to hunt.

This site appeared to still be in the developmental stages when we visited. The *Troodon Story* was a work-in-progress. *Dinosaur Dictionary* promised to be the most complete one on the Web but so far is not. This is, nevertheless, a nice site to visit, if only to meet the author.

Jobaria Home
www.jobaria.org

Jobaria, the Web site, was launched at 2 P.M. on November 11,
1999, simultaneously with the world debut of Jobaria, a new dinosaur giant from Africa. Jobaria guest-starred on *National Geographic's Explorer* on CNBC that same week. (Search for "Jobaria"
on www.nationalgeographic.com for video of the press conference
and of workers building the dinosaur, plus other related material.)
The Jobaria Web site is sponsored by Project Exploration (www.
projectexploration.org/). One of Project Exploration's missions is
to make the excitement of new dinosaur discoveries accessible to
the public, especially children. The organization sponsors hands-
on education for junior paleontologists, including a field trip to
Africa (www.projectexploration.org/JPBody.html) and future
plans for a field camp in the West.

Elegantly designed as an expedition, with passport and visa,
this site has four sections. The media are invited to *Orientation* for
press releases, photos, and images for use in publications, recent
articles, and links to other sites. It also includes a statement from
Project Exploration cofounders, paleontologist Paul Sereno (dino-
saur.uchicago.edu/) and educator Gabrielle Lyon, about the sale,
trade, and auction of dinosaur fossils. In the *Jobaria* section visitors
can learn more about what makes this dinosaur unique. See how
an elephant named Angus helped the team figure out whether or
not Jobaria could rear on its hind legs. An interactive skeleton gives
you a close-up of Jobaria's characteristic anatomy.

Build a Dinosaur is an illustrated step-by-step journey along the
route of building a dinosaur—from finding the bones in the Sahara
Desert to erecting the skeleton and sharing the discovery. Learn
about how Paul Sereno ran in the Chicago Marathon to raise money
to build the skeleton of Jobaria.

Background information about the 1997 expedition is available
on *The Expedition* page, including supply stat sheets, a route map,
biographies of team members, and diary excerpts from one of the

team members. (For instance, the field team used three pounds of garlic powder, 250 pounds of pasta [explaining the garlic powder], 41 pounds of Jolly Ranchers, 150 freeze-dried ice-cream sandwiches, 1,200 granola bars, and 600 rolls of toilet paper.) One of the highlights is the "Sahara Connection" exhibit, created from letters sent between Chicago public school children and expedition members during the 1997 expedition to Niger. Included in this area is a page on the African culture, particularly kente cloth and the meaning behind the patterns that can be woven into it.

Teacher Tracks is a collection of interdisciplinary, thought-provoking questions, activities, and classroom extensions designed for teachers and parents to use with students. *Where to Look* is an activity designed for grades six through eight that asks students to combine information from research reports, geology, and geographic maps to decide the best place to look for Cretaceous dinosaurs. This activity is based on the real site where Jobaria was discovered.

Jurassic Park: The Adventure
jurassic.unicity.com/

You are the new director of operations at Jurassic Park Hollywood. When the alarm sounds and people start running, you'll have to face the terror that awaits you in the labyrinth of halls and rooms inside the InGen complex. With no extra plug-ins required, all you'll need to play the *Online Experience* is a Java-enabled browser (MSIE 3.0 or above) and a 14.4 bps modem. A sound card is recommended to get the full Jurassic Park experience.

Kids will have no problem figuring out this game, but it may be a different story for adults. Read the *FAQs* or go to the *Intranet* for hints and clues. Sound effects and a scary *Velociraptor* make this a lot of fun.

The point of this site is to promote Jurassic Park—The Ride at Universal Studios. But what else is there?

Megalania Dinosaur Pages
members.tripod.com/~megalania/dinosaur.html

Here's a dinosaur lover with a sense of humor. At the top of this page is an animated dinosaur, offered as proof that the *Tyrannosaurus rex* could, indeed, run. At the top of *Megalania Dinosaur News Pages* is another animated dinosaur, flipping the pages of a newspaper, offered, we presume, as proof that dinosaurs could read. Dino news articles on this page range from a discussion of the dinosaur-bird connection from the *San Francisco Chronicle,* to a story from the Xinhua News Agency about the two thousand dinosaur eggs found in Spain.

In the *Dinosaurs in Popular Culture Pages,* see video captures of the showdown between King Kong and a huge, lizardlike tyrannosaur in the classic adventure movie *King Kong.* As Larry Dunn states, many of us started loving dinosaurs when we first saw that giant lizard locked in a life-and-death battle with King Kong. "We now know, of course, that tyrannosaurs didn't look anything like the one portrayed in the movie, but the creature has such personality and the combat is so exciting that it remains a real thrill to see," Dunn writes. The video captures are good enough for the Internet and are also fun to see.

Probably the best feature of this site are the reviews of dinosaur models in resin, vinyl, or styrene. See photographs of and comments on dinosaur sculptures in various scales by Menagerie Productions (Tony McVey); Maximos Salas's terrific *Thylacosmilus ferox,* the saber-toothed marsupial that stalked the Miocene pampas; David Krentz's gorgeous *Gorgosaurus libratus;* the Dinosaur Studio's strictly accurate dinosaur models; Matt Manit's accurate *Deinonychus;* a review of the *Prehistoric Times,* the popular magazine devoted to dinosaur models, toys, and other collector's items; Ray Rimell's new book, *Building and Painting Model Dinosaurs;* Geraths Illustration and Sculpture; Trcic Studio's dynamic dinosaur; and resin models of prehistoric reptile skulls and a very big fish by Wiccart's Steve

Harvey. Not all of these companies have Web sites, and so the Web author provides addresses and phone numbers, as well as prices.

As an added service, Dunn thumbs through all of the available television listings in search of programs on dinosaurs. You won't be able to find his weekly summaries on his Web site, but you can find them on the *Dinosaur Mailing List* (www.cmnh.org/fun/dinosaur-archive/index.html), sponsored by the Cleveland Museum of Natural History. The *Mailing List* advises to click on the current month and then click on *search by author* or *subject.* This feature is useless because there are so many titles to scroll through and scan. We found it easier to use our Web browser's search or "find in page" to find *Dinosaur TV Week,* after clicking on a month and a year. An amusing read, unless you are offended by barbs aimed at the Purple One.

The Mighty Triceratops Home Page
www.geocities.com/Area51/Lair/8113/

The Mighty Triceratops HomePage is "your one-stop source for *Triceratops* information." A massive herbivore of the Late Cretaceous Period, with a bony neck frill and three face horns, the *Triceratops* was one of the last and most numerous of dinosaurs. It was first discovered in 1889 near Denver, Colorado, in the Judith River Formation. *Triceratops* have also been found in the Lancian Formations of Wyoming, the Hell Creek area of Montana, the Scollard Formation of Saskatchewan, and the Red River Valley of Alberta. "Without doubt the most dangerous devices for active defense among the Dinosauria emerged in *Triceratops,*" writes Robert Bakker in *The Dinosaur Heresies.*

Interested in Trikes? On this site you'll find links to on-line encyclopedia articles, *Triceratops toys and collectibles, Triceratops in fiction and comics, Triceratops on the big (and small) screen,* an *Art Gallery, Articles and Info, Triceratops in Games,* a *Virtual Trike Museum,* preset links to search engines to *Web Search for Triceratops, The Mighty*

Trike's Kids' Section!, and *Trike Missing Links.* An eclectic collection of on-line Trike trivia.

National Geographic Home
www.nationalgeographic.com/

Naturally, nationalgeographic.com is as immense as the whole outdoors, and it has to be to keep up with its subject matter and multiple activities of the National Geographic Society. Web designers made sure this site is like an expedition—after all, why should the scientists, reporters, photographers, and producers have all the fun? Moreover, you won't need to lather on the sunscreen. A person could spend hours—no, weeks—exploring just this address. With all that is going on here, the state-of-the-art video, animation, photography, interactive activities, and tempting links, it is easy to get lost or frustrated with how much computer power it takes to navigate through all the different facets of the site. Take it from a veteran explorer, it is best to stick close to base camp, where all expeditions come together at www.nationalgeographic.com/.

At the top of Home @ nationalgeographic.com is the Site Index dropdown menu, which gives surfers starting places for everything that is available on the site. Shortcuts include: Shop Online, Interactive Features, Maps, Photography, News, Kids, Education, Forums, Live Events, Exhibitions, *National Geographic* magazine, *Traveler* magazine, *Adventure* magazine, *World* magazine, Books, *Explorer* on CNBC, National Geographic Channel, Expeditions (Travel), National Geographic Bee, and Research & Exploration. Nearly all of these separate Web pages will have something to offer about dinosaurs. Type in the word *dinosaurs,* or a more specific topic, to search the entire site for a list of everything that is still online. Former programs and news articles might also still be available.

The day we logged on, the Web site happened to feature an *Explorer* program about the latest dinosaur discoveries: Jobaria and Sue. We watched workers erecting Jobaria and its cousin at the museum, and viewed a video of a press conference (RealPlayer

or Windows plug-in required, although downloading can be done
from this site). Related to this single event were these nationalgeo-
graphic.com links: *Birdlike Dinosaur Discovered in Argentina* (press
event), *Dinorama @ nationalgeographic.com* (interactive feature),
Dinosaur Eggs @ nationalgeographic.com (interactive feature), *Dinosaur
Hunters* (video), *Dinosaurs of the Sahara* (exhibition), *Dinosaurs Are
Not Extinct: Their Descendants Fill the Sky* (news), *Feathered Dinosaurs*
(streaming-video lecture), *Fossils: Disappearing Treasures?* (news), *Fossils from China Link Birds with Dinosaurs* (press event), *Huge Dinosaur
Emerges from the Sahara* (press event), and *New Birdlike Dinosaurs
from China Are True Missing Links* (press event).

Dinorama @ nationalgeographic.com (www.nationalgeographic.
com/dinorama/) is a standing feature about . . . you guessed it. You
can choose from these categories: *Why Feathers? A T. Rex Called Sue,
History's Nursery, Moving Monsters, Desert Discovery, Dinosaur Eggs,*
and *Early Birds?* Each of these pages is cross-referenced with videos,
interactive activities, and articles offered elsewhere. You can see how
computer animators help scientists learn how dinosaurs might have
moved in *Moving Monsters.* In *Why Feathers?* you can view and rotate
a 3-D image of the dino-bird *Sinornithosaurus* (QuickTime required).
You can also go to a live image of "Feathers and Fossils: New Links in
Dinosaur Evolution" exhibited in *Explorer's Hall* (which is, by the way,
another page that is worth, well, exploring).

Venture into a *Dinosaur's Neighborhood* at *Family Xpeditions*
(www.nationalgeographic.com/xpeditions/). *Family Xpeditions* is a
multimedia feast that is similar to a video or CD-Rom game. There
are many activities to choose from, but the only drawback is that
there is no clear menu. To get to *Dinosaur's Neighborhood,* click on
Family Xpeditions, which will take you to the activities page featuring a random activity. A compass appears in the left-hand frame
labeled "Activities." Click on the Roman numeral II, which should
take you to *Dinosaur's Neighborhood.* Here, you can check out the
real estate (that is, if you were a dinosaur, would you prefer to live
on the coast or in a desert dream house?); view a map of the earth's
climate zones to figure out where dinosaurs would live today; or get
into a dinosaur's head by viewing a CT scan of a *T. rex.* (Some of
these features weren't working the day we visited.) This page links
to other pages previously discussed.

Another way to find dinosaur stuff on this Web site, especially for young children, is through *Kids @ nationalgeographic.com.* (www.nationalgeographic.com/kids/). This is a cartoon version of the home page, but at least you can get to a *Dinosaur's Neighborhood* and *Dino Eggs* from here.

Be sure to go to *National Geographic* magazine (month, year) @ nationalgeographic.com (www.nationalgeographic.com/ngm/) and NGNews @ nationalgeographic.com (www.ngnews.com/) for the latest magazine articles and news releases about dinosaurs.

National Geographic has done its best to use high technology to its fullest advantage, offering unique information and interaction that supplement, rather than merely repeat, magazine articles and television programs. However, with all the technology and information, the site is difficult to navigate and cumbersome, at times, to download. A fast computer with lots of memory and the latest plug-ins is required. Sometimes, users will have to defrag their computer before continuing with all of the components. Nevertheless, this site is one of the best we've seen.

Online Puzzles for Kids— Dinosaur Scrambler

www.edbydesign.com/scr_dino.html

Here's a chance to have fun while learning a little about dinosaurs. This page allows children of all ages to reassemble scrambled images of dinosaurs right on-line. Choose from one of nine images, like a *T. rex* or *Parasaurolophus,* and click on *Load.* Choose the level of difficulty: easy (nine squares), medium (twelve squares), and hard (sixteen squares). View the image and then select *Scramble.* Click on two titles to swap them around until the puzzle is solved. There is even a timer and a *Solve* button in case you get frustrated. Loads of fun.

Sir Arthur Conan Doyle's The Lost World
www.geocities.com/SoHo/9094/TheLostWorld.html

Famous for writing the adventures of the greatest fictional detective, Sherlock Holmes, Arthur Conan Doyle was renowned for his historical and romance novels, and ghost and spiritualist stories. *The Lost World*, one of Doyle's "Challenger Adventures," is the first novel to focus on dinosaurs and other prehistoric life. In fact, it is the proto-tale of a whole genre of dinosaur-related stories about a "lost world" scenario, where explorers discover a hidden land in which the laws of nature have been suspended. Many literary scholars feel that *The Lost World* may also rightfully be considered one of the greatest adventure stories ever written. *The Lost World* was originally published as a serialized story in the magazine *The Strand* from April to October 1912 (vols. 43 and 44).

Read an account of the history and the story elements of *The Lost World* on this Web site, as well as the entire novel. The first *Lost World* movie was not the 1992 version but was first filmed in 1925. Reviews, notes, and video purchase information are available here. There's also a collection of images relating to *The Lost World*, Victorian paleontology, etc., plus a special visit from the first lady of dinosaur cinema, Gertie the Dinosaur. *Articles* provides a collection of essays on *The Lost World*, while *Links* guide further journeys into *The Lost World*, Victorian paleontology, silent movies, FX master Willis O'Brien, and the world of Sir Arthur Conan Doyle.

A great site for Victorian dinosaur buffs and Sherlock fans!

Sir Arthur Conan Doyle's The Lost World—Television Series

www.thelostworldtv.com/home.html

The Lost World, Sir Arthur Conan Doyle's classic tale of dinosaurs and adventure, has been transformed into twenty-two hour-long episodes of original action set in the turn of the century. Shot on location in Australia, *The Lost World* tells the story of a mismatched British expedition team led by adventurer Prof. Edward Challenger, who is determined to prove the existence of an unknown age.

Near the end of their treacherous river journey, the expedition is forced to escape a sudden tribal attack in their hot-air balloon, which crash-lands on the eerie plateau of the Lost World. The team is trapped in this exotic land, where they face unfamiliar danger at every turn. Vicious packs of ape-men, giant crocodiles, bizarre plant life, and flesh-eating dinosaurs test the group's resolve and threaten their return home. In order to survive in this untamed environment, the expedition must rely on Veronica, a beautiful stranger who has raised herself alone in the land of the dinosaurs. Her unique knowledge of this world is the team's only chance to stay alive and perhaps find a way to return home.

This Web site meets all expectations of a high-end production—handsome design with the feel of a Victorian scientific expedition and computer-animated Hollywood FX. Here you will meet the characters, explore the Lost World, read about the episodes, and go behind the scenes. *Behind the Scenes* is literally behind a door, where you'll learn about how the dinosaurs and creatures were wrangled, locations, props, production, computer-generated effects, and even makeup. You can download exciting scenes for wallpaper or theme music, or send an episodic post card to a friend within the *Adventure Zone.* Unfortunately, the television episode does not do justice to Doyle's original work.

This site requires a Flash 4 plug-in and QuickTime to play the videos.

Unnatural Museum Dinosaur Safari
unmuseum.mus.pa.us/dinosaf.htm

The Museum of Unnatural History is an on-line virtual museum that takes a unique and sometimes bizarre look at dinosaurs. You'll need your 3-D glasses to view some of the dinosaur images along the way. Just click on the red-and-blue glasses icon at the top or bottom of every page for the featured 3-D picture. Don't have 3-D glasses? You can also view a stereoscopic image, for which there's an icon on every page, as well. (See unmuseum.mus.pa.us/3d.htm for more information on 3-D and duo-image glasses.)

Lee Krystek begins Dinosaur Safari by laying the groundwork: What's a dinosaur? What's a fossil? Extinction ("Who Dunnit?"), and dinosaur metabolism (including the "Hot and Cold Running Dinosaurs" controversy). The point of this Web site, however, is to expose the myths about dinosaurs that have evolved in popular culture over the last two centuries with the help of moviemakers, authors, magicians, and early publicity-seeking "scientists."

Victorian Dinosaurs discusses how dinosaurs were discovered and what people thought of them in the nineteenth century. We can thank Richard Owen, who in 1846 coined the term *Dinosauria,* from the Greek for "terrible lizard," though they were certainly different from any lizards we see today. Drawings of these huge lizards fired the imagination of nineteenth-century scientists and the general public alike. This article tells some amusing stories of English royalty and pompous scientists. *Doyle's Trick* tells the story of the prank that Sir Arthur Conan Doyle, author of *The Lost World,* pulled on his friend and famous magician, Harry Houdini, and the Society of Magicians.

Another fascination of the general public is the question of whether dinosaurs still exist today (as a matter of fact they do— as birds). In *Reptiles of the Ancient Seas,* the Loch Ness Monster and other sea serpent possibilities are explored. "Dinosaurs in the Congo," the tale of *mok_ele-nbembe,* is told on the page called *The*

Legend of the African Dinosaur, and giant birds are examined in "Pterosaurs in Texas" on the *Flying Reptiles in Texas* page.

If no dinosaurs are alive today, why have we seen them in the movies for years? Lee Krystek discusses *Stop Motion Photography,* which enabled moviemakers to animate models of Godzilla and other monsters. Of course, that was before the age of computer graphic manipulation.

Could someone actually build a Jurassic Park in today's world? Click on the *Dinosaur DNA* link and you'll find a step-by-step recipe for making a dinosaur. Step 1: Find amber with mosquito in it. Step 2: Extract dino blood from insect. Step 3: Create blueprints from genetic code found in the dino blood, fill in with frog DNA as needed. Steps 4, 5, 6, and 7: Create a dino egg from the blueprints, hatch, raise to full size, and enjoy. Is this really possible? The Web author examines the ingredients in the recipe.

The Museum of Unnatural History isn't just about dinosaurs. An incredible journey is awaiting surfers at unmuseum.mus.pa.us/. Not connected to the Dinosaur Safari pages, the *Lost Worlds Exhibition* is relevant to many of the topics discussed in the dinosaur pages. Lost Worlds is about cryptozoology, or the study and research of previously unknown or hidden animals. Another great place to visit, and sometimes relevant to the subject of dinosaurs, is *Science Over the Edge,* a monthly page on strange science news. Other features include the *Hall of UFO Mysteries* (about "things people see in the sky they shouldn't"), *A Collection of Odd Archaeology,* a *Children's Reading Room,* and *Mad Scientist's Laboratory,* for experiments you can do at home. In *The Virtual Cyclorama,* you will visit distant and long-forgotten places through this fusion of twenty-first-century technology and nineteenth-century ingenuity (Java plug-in required). The options are endless. To see these other Web pages, click on the Home button at the bottom of every page within the above address. Did we mention the music to surf by?

This is a vast, well-organized, visually exciting, wacky presentation of good, old-fashioned scientific thinking.

Unofficial Dinosaurs Home Page
www.sci.kun.nl/thalia/funpage/television/dinosaurs/

This is an unofficial Web site about Jim Henson's *The Dinosaurs* in syndication on the Disney Channel, a puppet situation comedy that was canceled after sixty-five episodes. The Unofficial Dinosaurs Homepage summarizes the show, characters, episodes, and the actors who gave their voices to the puppets. The site also provides RealAudio and RealVideo zipped downloads of some of the episodes, as well as a number of color JPG images of the characters. Search for *The Dinosaurs* on Jim Henson's official Web site at www.henson.com.

Zoom Dinosaurs—Enchanted Learning Software
www.EnchantedLearning.com/subjects/dinosaurs/

Enchanted Learning produces children's educational Web sites and games designed to capture the imagination while maximizing creativity, learning, and enjoyment. *Zoom School* (www.Enchanted Learning.com/school/) is an on-line elementary school classroom with lessons in geography, biology, language arts, and early childhood activities. Listed in the *Zoom School* index is *Zoom Dinosaurs,* a comprehensive on-line hypertextbook about dinosaurs. It is designed for students of all ages and levels of comprehension. It has an easy-to-use structure that allows readers to start at a basic level on each topic, and then to progress to much more advanced information as desired, simply by clicking on links.

Links on Zoom Dinosaurs include: *All About Dinosaurs, Dino News, Dino Info Sheets, Dino Printouts, List of Dinos, Anatomy & Behavior, Mesozoic Era, Extinction, Fossils, Plants, Classification, Dino Quizzes, Dino Dictionary, Classroom Activities, Ask a Question, Dino Fun,* and *Geologic Time Chart.*

All About Dinosaurs defines the dinosaur, provides 105 dinosaur information sheets on *Apatosaurus, Tyrannosaurus, Triceratops, Velociraptor,* and many more, as well as thirty-seven labeled, black-and-white dinosaur printouts. It discusses how dinosaurs are named, evolution, extinction, birds and dinosaurs, and dinosaur myths created by Hollywood. *Record Breakers* is about the biggest, the smallest, the fastest, the tallest, the widest, the smartest, the oldest, the most plated, the strongest skulled, biggest clawed, longest lived, longest neck or tailed, the deadliest, and the largest eggs. The dinosaur classification process is thoroughly explained in terms the elementary student can understand. The time periods and fossils are the subject matter for a number of units. The illustrated *Dinosaur Dictionary* has more than one thousand entries: hundreds of dinosaurs and other ancient life-forms, paleontological and geology terms, and biographies on the great paleontologist fossil hunters of all time. Dinosaur jokes, games, puzzles, quizzes, crafts, fun activities, and art can be found here, as well as lessons in how to write a funny dinosaur poem or a great school report on dinosaurs. *Dino News* publishes up-to-the-minute articles about dinosaurs in language that is easy for younger children to understand.

Colorful, fast loading, and well organized, researched, and written, this is a must for any elementary school teacher. And the cost is affordable—free!

Barney-Online
barneyonline.com/

You knew we had to include Barney. This is a sweet, cartoon-animated Web site that will either delight you and your children, or not—depending upon your point of view. Click on *Playtime,* type in your first name or screen name, and go into the tree house for music (RealPlayer required), storytime, books, mail (for pretend letters from Barney), and art fun. Click on *Store* for books, video, toys, audio CDs and tapes, and *Barney's Watch, Play & Learn,* an activity guide for parents and child-care providers. This book contains more than four hundred simple, creative ideas that help young children discover and learn all about themselves and their world. You can join Barney's Buddie Club in *Store*. Click on *Barney News* for details of some of the upcoming shows. Use a search engine such as Yahoo. com to find a plethora of sites on Barney, pro and con.

CHAPTER 2

DINO FACTS

ABCNEWS.com: Science Index
abcnews.go.com/sections/science/

ABCNEWS.com regularly keeps up with the dinosaur beat. The day we logged on, the top story on this page was "The Unchanging Dinosaur," about the sixty-foot-long sauropod found in Africa that stayed the same for forty million years, as compared to a close cousin who had a face like Darth Vader and six hundred teeth. You will need RealPlayer to view the linked film; you can download the latest version from the site. The article itself is nicely illustrated with sketches and photographs. A search on "dinosaurs" in the site's search engine revealed more than three hundred timely articles, one hundred of which were sorted by date. Bookmark this site for your daily news on dinosaurs.

Academic Press Encyclopedia of Dinosaurs
www.apnet.com/dinosaur/dinopen.htm

This Web site was designed to promote *Encyclopedia of Dinosaurs,* edited by Dr. Philip Currie of the Royal Tyrrell Museum of Paleontology, Alberta, Canada, and Dr. Kevin Padian, of the Museum of Paleontology, University of California. It is a reference work that provides accurate, comprehensive information to professionals in this field and also to the interested public. The encyclopedia

includes 275 different articles providing a wide-ranging picture of
the current scholarly research on dinosaurs. The articles were written by a group of more than one hundred authors, including virtually
all of the prominent authorities in this field. The entries cover eleven
general subject areas and range from extended articles of more than
ten pages in length on major themes to capsulized entries of one
paragraph on specific issues. The articles are illustrated by black-
and-white and full-color artwork. The Web site gives a complete list
of articles and their authors and twenty sample articles ranging from
information on the Dinosaur Society to the histology of teeth. As an
added bonus, you can read Michael Crichton's foreword to the book
in total.

The Age of Dinosaurs (BIOL 1090)
Course Outline at
Nova Southeastern University
www.nova.edu/ocean/biol1090/W-DINO-SYLLABUS.htm

We've included this course syllabus because we thought you'd find
it interesting to see the inside of a college-level course on dinosaurs.
This one, in particular, reads like a well-written book. Here is an
example of this Web author's wit:

> *Dinosaur* also has an unfortunate connotation: something
> impractically large, out-of-date or obsolete; unwieldy and out-
> moded. Such usage is really no longer justifiable based on what
> we now know about these remarkable animals. So, calling your
> boss, car or refrigerator a dinosaur should no longer have the
> same negative implication that it used to.

The course is called "The Age of Dinosaurs." It is an introduction to the most fascinating period of life on earth—the Mesozoic
Era—emphasizing the most famous inhabitants of the time—the
dinosaurs: their kinds, ecology, evolution, life habits, and eventual
extinction. The course also introduces basic concepts of scientific

thinking, evolution, geology, and paleontology needed to understand dinosaurs, as well as the other animals and plants that populated the Mesozoic world.

Ordovician Conodonts
www.geocities.com/CapeCanaveral/Hall/1383/2TopCone.htm

What are conodonts? They are "cone teeth" as vicious-looking as any tyrannosaur jawbone, but ten times older—and no larger than a grain of sand. These microscopic, ancient objects were deposited in sediments during the Paleozoic Era between a quarter billion and half a billion years ago and can be found in ordinary dirt—possibly in your own backyard. Their small size and durable chemical composition allowed them to survive millions of years nearly unchanged.

These rare fossils show that the original owner of the conodont was an eel-like animal, whose teeth clustered together to form an oddly shaped jaw. The eel may have been related to modern backboned animals, but there is no animal living today that has a set of choppers quite like these, and paleontologists are uncertain what creature left them behind.

Conodonts are easy to find and fascinating to study. Jim Davison, an amateur paleontologist and emergency room doctor, found them in his own backyard in Nashville, Tennessee, and studies them for a hobby. He uses his Web site to organize and display his collection, allowing others to enjoy their uniqueness. He displays remarkable photographs of more than forty specimens on his site. Instructions for finding the conodonts and taking their pictures are posted there. You can look in on his research in progress, and E-mail him with suggestions.

Dinofish.com—Coelacanth: The Fish Out of Time

www.dinofish.com/

The coelacanth (pronounced see-la-kanth), a four-hundred-million-year-old "living fossil" fish, was once thought to have gone extinct with the dinosaurs. Technically, this fish is neither a dinosaur nor extinct. In 1938 a fishing trawler off the coast of South Africa caught in its net a grouper-size fish of unknown description. Fish experts regard the fish to be a member of the coelacanth family, partly because of its triple-lobed tail, although it was thought to have become extinct sixty-five million years earlier. A second was discovered by an English fishing captain off the coast of the Comero Islands.

Over the decades many expeditions, led by prominent scientists, television programs, and royalty, were launched in the Comero Islands to obtain a second specimen. Although the fish was photographed and nearly trapped by natives, these attempts to obtain a specimen for study failed. Forty-six years after the discovery of the Comero Islands coelacanths, a new population was identified off the coast of North Sulawesi, Indonesia. Honeymooners snapped a picture of a specimen being wheeled through a fish market. A year later, a second was caught; it died despite efforts to keep it alive. This new species, thought to be a deep-reef fish, has been named *Latimeria menadoensis*. It is believed that a population in the low hundreds still exists in the world today.

Further details of the expedition history, biology, and behavior are available on Dinofish.com. A fast-loading "virtual swimming coelacanth" is featured on the site; its combination of four flapping legs and three fins makes it look like a ship's propeller. To raise funds for the preservation of this endangered fish, documentary videos, T-shirts, and the like are sold on this Web site. A fascinating read for those interested in the theory that dinosaurs still live among us.

Dinosaur Reference Center
www.crl.com/~sarima/dinosaurs/

Dinosaur Reference Center provides a list of the different types of dinosaurs and their relatives, which is called "taxonomy." Taxonomy is the science of classifying organisms in a natural framework. Not all scientists agree on the same ways to classify dinosaurs. The author, Stanley Friesen, defines the different kinds of taxonomy, and gives the reasons why he prefers the "evolutionary" or "traditional" taxonomy over other systems. He then lists his preferred classifications of dinosaurs as well as an index of all known dinosaurs, alphabetized by genus. The list includes names of fragmentary or otherwise doubtful forms, called *nomina dubia*. New dinosaurs are rapidly discovered all the time and written about in obscure scientific journals, and so Stanley Friesen's list is incomplete but updated regularly. He includes a *What's New* page for additions to his lists.

The information is presented in a concise, scientific manner, and includes short notes on the more technical terms and the author's opinions. There are no bells and whistles or fancy artwork to this site, except for the illustration of the "really, really fat ankylosaur"—and really cute, we might add. Navigating this site is simply done by following the helpful arrows. A must-see for middle and high school biology students.

Dinosaurs Alive! Home Page
www.onlineclass.com/Dinosaurs/

OnlineClass has created teaching units on a select variety of topics, which allow you to use the Internet as a communications and research tool. Dinosaurs Alive! is one interactive Internet class that uses dinosaurs to teach scientific research techniques and to share science as an ongoing process, specifically for grades kindergarten through six, readers and nonreaders alike. The course focuses on a different aspect of dinosaur research in each unit and gives students a chance to uncover facts and form hypotheses themselves, as each classroom "adopts" a dinosaur species and works to research its animal in the library and on the World Wide Web.

As students hear from guest scientists about the process of discovery, digging, preserving, studying, and displaying dinosaurs, they will become familiar with the latest tools, technologies, and theories related to dinosaurs. Unit inquiry themes stimulate individual creativity and challenge students to do their own research and participate in in-class and extended learning activities. Students' artwork, models, essays, poems, and other creative works are displayed on a Web site built and maintained for each school.

Dinosaurs Alive! on-line sessions are offered four times a year. Each session has seven study units, which take place within a ten-week interactive quarter. Teachers can stretch all seven units over the ten weeks, or come and go as their schedule allows. Program features and descriptions of each class are available on www.onlineclass. com/Dinosaurs/features.htm. This page links to sample unit pages.

Here is a brief breakdown of the first three units of the program: Unit 1: Dinos Defined—What is a dinosaur? The major dinosaur features and the geological time scale need to be defined before each class can adopt a dinosaur for further research. Unit 2: Dino World!—Where did the dinosaurs live and what was their world like? A quick look at the locations of dinosaurs and the climate. During this unit, classrooms will adopt their dinosaur from a given list, and the classroom research will begin. Unit 3:—We Dig Dinos! What is a paleontologist? How do they find dinosaurs, and how is it possible that new discoveries are being made after all these years?

Dinosaurs Alive! is a profit-making venture with reasonable pricing scaled to the number of students using the product, be it homeschooling families, a class of fewer than ten, or multiple classes totaling more than 151 students. At a modest price, it is also available to one administrator of a school for preview purposes only.

Dinosaurs: Facts and Fiction
pubs.usgs.gov/gip/dinosaurs/

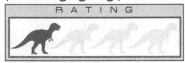

Dinosaurs: Facts and Fiction is a complete, on-line version of a printed pamphlet that is one of a series of general-interest publications prepared by the U.S. Geological Survey to provide information about the earth sciences, natural resources, and the environment. The site states that the study of dinosaurs is important for understanding the causes of past major extinctions of land animals, as well as for understanding the changes in biological diversity caused by previous geological and climatic changes of the earth. These changes are still occurring today. Scientists have discovered a wealth of new information about dinosaurs over the past thirty years, and old ideas of dinosaurs as slow, clumsy beasts have been totally turned around.

This pamphlet contains answers to some frequently asked questions about dinosaurs, with current ideas and evidence to correct some long-lived popular misconceptions. Although much has been discovered recently about dinosaurs, there is still a great deal more to learn about our planet and its ancient inhabitants. This site does not contain information that cannot be found elsewhere, but it is interesting to note that it exists and is a good resource for quick school papers. Some graphics displayed.

Dinosaur Trace Fossils
www.emory.edu/COLLEGE/ENVS/research/ichnology/dinotraces.html

If all of the dinosaur bones in the world were to disappear tomorrow, paleontologists would still have plenty of evidence for the existence of dinosaurs through "trace fossils." Proof that dinosaurs existed lies in the fossilized bones and impressions of their bones and skin. Dinosaurs left trace fossils as tracks, tooth marks, eggs, nests, gastroliths (small stones formed in the stomach), and coprolites (dung). Take note of the background of this Web page, a Thalassinoides, or burrow network, probably formed by an arthropod in a shallow marine environment like an ocean bed.

A trace fossil is indirect evidence of ancient life. In contrast, a body fossil is direct evidence of ancient life that involves some body part of the organism. Skin impressions are not trace fossils unless they were made while the dinosaur was still alive, such as the imprint made by a footstep. The Dinosaur Trace Fossils Web site discusses tracks and trackways, eggs and nests, tooth marks, gastroliths, and coprolites on separate Web pages. Each subject is illustrated with interesting photographs that don't take long to download.

Dr. Anthony "Tony" Martin teaches environmental geology, earth history, and paleontology at Emory University. There's a picture of him on his biography page posing next to the skeletal reconstruction of a *T. rex*. That's him in the foreground, he says, in case you couldn't tell the difference between the scary poses. His research specialty is trace fossils, and he believes this site is the only comprehensive one in this field. The Web site is written in an easy-to-understand manner for use by anyone interested in dinosaurs, whether students or the general public. He also provides lists of books on trace fossils. Follow the *Emory University Trace Fossils and Ichnology* (ichnology is the study of plant and animal traces) for updates to his site and an outline of the course he teaches. Each outline topic links to more fascinating stuff, like a newsletter on plant and animal traces and a database of the fossil traces Tony Martin "has known and loved."

Dinosaur Tracks from Holyoke, Massachusetts

members.aol.com/dinoprints/index.html

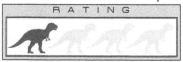

All Gary Gaulin wanted in his backyard was a fish pond. Instead, he discovered a two-hundred-million-year-old trackway site on his property in Holyoke, Massachusetts. The landowner knew in advance that the shale he was excavating occasionally contained trace fossils, and he was on the lookout for them as excavations began. He found trackways of *Grallator* and *Anchisauripus* under the very first continuous layer of strata. Under that layer were yet more trackways. Further examination indicated that there were trackways at intervals of every few inches or so. It is rare for there to be multiple layers of tracks so densely stacked. Usually, there are only two or three layers, but this site was a trackway sandwich!

Now Gary Gaulin is a backyard paleontologist. You can read his essay on his unique hypothesis for bird flight, see pictures of the trackways, and read other publicity articles about his discovery on his Web site.

Dinosaurussen-gids
(The Dutch Dinosaur Guide)
home.wxs.nl/~rsc32px7/home.html
Dutch version: Dinosaurus.net/

Originally authored in Dutch, this site is being translated into English, page by page. This is another complete encyclopedia-type site with all of the typical topics: What is a dinosaur? origin, anatomy, time line, warm- or cold-blooded, classification, the bird link, eggs and nests. Although it isn't clear, the author appears to be a paleo-artist, describing his methods of reconstructing his dinosaurs from bones to flesh on *Dino Reconstruction*. This site is well organized and navigable, and the beautiful, colorful illustrations are worthwhile.

Fossil News—Journal of Amateur Paleontology
www.fossilnews.com/

Fossil News—Journal of Amateur Paleontology is a monthly magazine published specifically with the fossil enthusiast or amateur paleontologist in mind. A wide variety of articles is presented, mostly by amateur paleontologists, on subjects ranging from field experiences to fossils of a given type or region to paleo-art to evolutionary theory. Whether you are an armchair paleontologist or an experienced field collector, there's something for you. In addition to the feature articles, the magazine offers book reviews, summaries of the latest findings reported in the primary literature, and a marketplace, where fossils, books, paleo-art, and services are advertised for sale and trade.

The title *Journal of Amateur Paleontology* does not imply that the staff and writers are not knowledgeable. "Amateur" merely means that the staff does this as an avocation, or for the love of it. Many of the writers have advanced degrees in related fields; just as many do not have degrees, but do have many years of applicable experience. Yet the magazine claims to strive to write in such a way that the neophyte and the lifelong paleophile can both find something of interest.

This is a subscription magazine that can be read on-line and printed out or brought to your house by snail mail at a much higher cost. Recently, the journal has added the option to download the newsletter in PDF (Portable Document Format), which requires Adobe Acrobat Reader, a free software that takes about twenty minutes to download. This allows you to print out the newsletter in its original print format.

You can try an issue for free by submitting an e-form provided on-line. The entire January 2000 fifth anniversary issue has been posted permanently on this site for all to see. Topics in this issue include: "A Short Paleontological Stroll in North Texas," "Ruben Dispels Rumors," "Rhino!!! (part 1)," "The Hypostome and I," "Ceratopsidae," "Masiln Beach, South Australia," "Dinosaur Collectibles," "Paleo-Humor," and a regular column called, "Bone Bug

Journal." You can also view back issues and read one article from
each issue in its entirety.

Graduate Programs in Vertebrate Paleontology
www.med.jhu.edu/FAE/weishampel/grad.html

The Education Committee of the Society of Vertebrate Paleontology has assembled a list of graduate programs from around the
world where studies in vertebrate paleontology can be pursued and
where support funds (research and stipend) can be obtained. The
list includes information about each program, along with mailing
addresses, E-mail addresses, and Internet links, to make it easier
for undergraduate students to make their decisions about graduate
schools. The list is not intended to be exhaustive but is likely to grow
as existing graduate programs make more use of electronic media
and as new programs come into being. So stay tuned to this site.

Hadrosaurus foulkii: Discovering the World's First Full Dinosaur Skeleton
www.levins.com/dinosaur.html

Dinosaurs in New Jersey too? Most definitely. In the summer of
1858, Victorian gentleman and fossil hobbyist William Parker
Foulke discovered the first nearly complete skeleton of a dinosaur in
a marl pit in Haddonfield, New Jersey. The discovery of the *Hadrosaurus foulkii* would rock the scientific world and forever change our
view of natural history.

Web site author Hoag Levin, incidentally, is the executive editor
of APBnews.com, a national news Web site focused on crime, justice, and safety issues. "In relation to the history of paleontology, the
physical Haddonfield *Hadrosaurus* site is ground zero; the spot where

our collective fascination with dinosaurs began," he writes. "Visitors can still climb down crude paths into the thirty-foot, vine-entangled chasm to stand in an almost primordial quiet at the actual marl pit where the imagination of all mankind was exploded outward to embrace the stunning fact that our planet was once ruled by fantastically large, bizarrely shaped reptilian creatures."

This Web site article has twelve sections, including *Into the Ravine Today, Finding the Bones in 1858, The Meaning of the Find, The Creature, Changing Shape of Hadrosaurus, Re-establishing the Site, 1984, Official State Fossil Designation, 1991: National Historic Site Designation, 1994: Dedication Ceremony, 1995: Maps: Haddonfield and Hadrosaurus Site,* and *Philadelphia Academy of Natural Sciences* (where the Haddonfield *Hadrosaurus foulkii* is displayed). To round out your cyber or physical visit to the Haddonfield hadrosaur site, Hoag Levin has added reviews of related books, as well as a guide to Haddonfield's restaurants, taverns, museums, shops, and events.

Lara's Dinosaur Page
www.pixelforge.net/odosbucket/dinosaurs.html

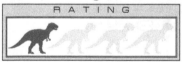

If you're interested in hadrosaurs, the duck-billed dinosaurs, you've come to the right place. They were a childhood fascination for the author of this Web site. She has dug for the bones of the *Maiasaura* (Good Mother Lizard) in Montana with the Paleontology Field School sponsored by the Museum of the Rockies, working alongside paleontologist John Horner. The purpose of this site is to provide a bibliography of sources devoted to, or with specific information on, hadrosaurs. By no means an exhaustive bibliography, it is extensive and includes a wide variety of sources that contain, in the opinion of the author, the best information. Each entry includes a short description.

As an added treat, the author includes *Amusing Dinodigging Songs:* "Day-o, day-o, daylight come and me want to dig bones."

NASA Classroom of the Future
www.cotf.edu/

The Classroom of the Future (COTF) program provides America's classrooms with the expertise of scientists from the National Aeronautics and Space Administration's (NASA), who have advanced the frontiers of knowledge in virtually every field of science over the last forty years. The COTF program is administered by the Erma Ora Byrd Center for Educational Technologies at Wheeling Jesuit University in Wheeling, West Virginia.

The COTF serves as NASA's premier research and development program for educational technologies. In this capacity the COTF develops and conducts research on technology-based learning materials that challenge students to solve problems by using data sets and other information resources provided by the four strategic enterprises of NASA: Aero-Space Technology, Human Exploration and Development of Space, Earth Science Enterprise, and Space Science.

One of the products COTF offers is Exploring the Environment, which includes lessons on dinosaurs. Exploring the Environment (ETE) consists of seventeen Web-based learning modules that address real environmental dilemmas worldwide. Students are trained on-line to use "imaging" software to help them use NASA's view from space to observe biological, chemical, and geological changes over enormous portions of the earth. Working in teams like real scientists, students are challenged to track a live hurricane, predict the global impact of a volcanic eruption, investigate the shrinking habitat of the mountain gorillas in Rwanda, and examine issues and images of the Amazon rain forest. ETE has received honors from Pacific Bell, the Geological Society of Canada, *Reader's Digest*, and numerous other organizations. For more information about Exploring the Environment, visit the product's Web site at www.cotf.edu/ete/.

Click on *Middle School Earth Science Explorer* from the above address to view the earth science and dinosaur museum, designed as a building. Take the elevator to the second floor to meet the dinosaurs and for information about the different or interconnecting disasters that may have caused their extinction. There is a Web page on *Shortcuts to Problem Solving,* but teachers will have to register for a password to view teaching guides.

Neil Clark's Home Page
www.gla.ac.uk/~gxha14/index.html

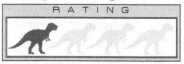

Neil Clark, curator of Paleontology at the Hunterian Museum in Glasgow, found the first trackway in Scotland on the Isle of Skye in 1996. The tracks are similar to the Triassic–Lower Jurassic trackways of Connecticut and are called *Grallator* and *Eubrontes* tracks. The Scottish find is in rocks of the Middle Jurassic Period. Scotland's first dinosaur was discovered on the Isle of Skye in 1992. The sauropod was nicknamed "Dougie the Dinosaur." The Web site lists fossils found at sites where Neil has worked, some discussion on Scottish geology, and links to museums and societies in Scotland.

According to the BBC, in September 1999, Neil released information on other fossilized bones recently recovered from a beach on the Isle of Skye in Scotland. These bones came from a species of stegosaur older than any previously known. The remains date from the Middle Jurassic Period, about 170 million years ago, and fill in a missing period in the evolution of this major dinosaur group. It was apparently the first bone ever found in the world of this particular dinosaur. We await additions on this discovery to his Web site.

New Scientist
www.newscientist.com/

The *New Scientist,* a weekly science magazine out of London, England, publishes some of its articles on-line. It features a regular dinosaur column called "The Rex Files." From the home page, click on *The Rex Files* for introductory information on *Tyrannosaurus rex*. This page links to other relevant topics, some of which you've read about before but not quite from this point of view: *Dinosauria, T-rex, What Killed Them?; Dino DNA, Were They Warm-Blooded?; From Birds to Dinos;* and *Thieves and Dealers*. Each of these pages is a subcategory of sorts, and you will find more links to recent articles on each subject. For instance, *Thieves and Dealers* will lead to "*T. rex* Raiders," "Big Feet," "What Am I Bid for This *T. rex?*" "Pssst . . . Wanna a Tryceratops?" and "US Bill Could Give Fossil Hunters a Field Day." Back on the contents page, click on the link beneath *The Rex Files* icon for the most recent article. The site also has a search engine, but results will include *all* of the pages where the word appears, whether relevant or not.

Newton's Apple Index/PBS
ericir.syr.edu/Projects/Newton/

Newton's Apple has posted lessons from the teacher's guides developed for seasons 9 through 15, five of which involve dinosaurs. They are designed to accompany the television show and are also a rich stand-alone resource. *Dinosaur I,* "Finding and Dating" (ericir.syr.edu/Projects/Newton/9/dino1.html), and *Dinosaur II,* "Assembling a Dinosaur" (ericir.syr.edu/Projects/Newton/9/dino2. html), were created to accompany show no. 906 in season 9. In season 12, *Movie Dinosaurs,* "How did they make the Jurassic Park dinosaur?" (ericir.syr.edu/Projects/Newton/12/Lessons/moviedino. html), was created for show no. 1205, and *Dinosaur Extinction,* "Where did the dinosaurs go?" (ericir.syr.edu/Projects/Newton/ 12/Lessons/dinoextn.html), was created for show no. 1207. Finally, *The Lost World Dinosaurs,* "How were dinosaurs created for Jurassic Park: The Ride" (ericir.syr.edu/Projects/Newton/15/lostworld.html), was created for show no. 1501, season 15.

Here is a sneak preview of *The Lost World Dinosaurs:* Scientists extrapolated dinosaur movements and posture by studying the size and shape of bones and connective tissue, and by observing the layout of fossils of dinosaurs that had apparently died while still running or fighting. Robotics experts at a defense contractor then modeled these movements with an advanced hydraulic technology first developed for the space program.

Try this: Raise your arm or leg and notice what other parts of your body shift or move also. Is this movement consistent? Can you move a limb without moving any other part of your body?

Rather than a glamorous electronic feat (all of Newton's Apple ingenuity goes into broadcasting), these pages look like they're right out of a teacher's guide—but that doesn't make them any less worthwhile. (Site design does improve with each season.) Each lesson contains talking points, more recently called "Insights and Connections," a vocabulary list, resource list, and "Try This" activities.

NOVA Online/Curse of the T. rex
www.pbs.org/wgbh/nova/trex/

"Curse of the T. Rex" first aired on *Nova*, PBS, in early 1997, but it rebroadcasts periodically. This program follows the trail of legal and illegal dealings in fossils as the FBI tries to protect the best *Tyrannosaurus rex* specimen (dubbed Sue by the team that discovered the remains) ever found from winding up on the shelves of a souvenir shop. Explore the colorful cast of animals and plants that lived alongside the dinosaurs in *The Dinosaurs Weren't Alone*. Find out how dinosaur hunters know where to begin looking in *Where to Dig (Hot Science)*. *Teacher's Guide* is a classroom activity that engages students in the legalities and excitement of finding a fossil. A complete transcript is available by following a link on the *Table of Contents*. This was a top-of-the-Web site in its day, but technology has surpassed it, as evidenced on similar television-magazine sites. However, it is still a valuable bookmark.

Pachycephalosauria: "Bone Heads"
www.geocities.com/Athens/Styx/3406

Pachycephalosaurus was a dome-headed dinosaur. Its huge head housed an incredibly thick skull, a tiny brain, and large eyes. It grew to be about 15 feet long (4.6 m) and may have weighed roughly 950 pounds (430 kg). It had short forelimbs and a stiff tail, with a distinctive mesh of interwoven tendons surrounding its rear portion. Bumpy knobs adorned its snout and the rear of its skull. This plant-eater probably had a good sense of smell and was a herding dinosaur that lived in small groups in coastal and upland regions.

Pachycephalosauria: "bone heads" was erected to support the study of these specific dinosaurs, and it tries to give children and adults a more complete vision of this amazing group of dinosaurs. Here you will find all the latest bits of news concerning discoveries, theories, statements, and research about the *Pachycephalosauria.* The site gives a list of all the specimens referred to as the respective species of the *Pachycephalosauria,* although all of the links for each specimen are dead.

The paleobiology section discusses the food consumption of the pachycephalosaurs, weights and lengths, speed and gait, brain, and sexual selection. The site also offers a time scale, glossary, references, and a history of discovery from the first tooth found in 1856 in Montana. The Web author explores the argument of whether the *Pachycephalosaurus,* with its ten-inch skull, was a head-butter.

A site for scholars of the lesser-known but interesting dinosaur.

Paleo Mont Park
www.geocities.com/CapeCanaveral/Lab/7634/

Paleo Mont Park is a one-man operation run by Kelly Wicks, a biology student at Dickinson State University in North Dakota. The bold objective of Paleo Mont is to "preserve fossils, through research and preservation of the paleontological past." Kelly's Bone Bed (KBB) is the focus of Paleo Mont, located in the Judith River Formation (Basin). Kelly claims to have collected ceratopsian caudal vertabrae and hadrosaurid vertabrae, tarsals, rib bones, leg bones, and scapulae. See *Collections* and *Fossil Pictures* for more detailed descriptions of these finds.

Another Web page within this site, titled *Paleo Mont's Timescale Adventure,* is a ten-day journal of a dig he went on one summer, sponsored by Timescale Adventures (timescale.3rivers.net). He worked on a tyrannosaurid/hadrosaurid site and uncovered several new fossils himself. One day he dug and collected a tooth and ribs, and "jacketed" another tyrannosaur tarsal. He goes into more detail of how to dig extinct animals and dinosaurs in a talk he gave, "Tools for Triceratops," reprinted on a Web page called *Makoshika*. Finally, he gives a useful list of equipment needed to execute a successful dig. This includes various hammers, chisels, spades, trowels, and brushes; surveying tools like a survey grid, measuring tape, and pegs; plasters, resins; sunscreen, hat, water. Most important, he advises, remember to obtain the landowner's permission.

This site was created by a young man who is at the beginning of his paleontological education (the site hasn't been updated since 1998) and whose enthusiasm is contagious. Not a site for finding unknown information about dinosaurs, but definitely come here for encouragement to step away from the computer and into the field.

And trust him about the sunscreen.

Paleontology in North Dakota
www.state.nd.us/ndfossils

RATING

North Dakota Geological Survey's Web site on paleontology was just getting under way when we went to press, but its genesis proved so promising that we had to include it in this review. What's so special about North Dakota? Well, for one thing, the top of the Hell Creek Formation, the only dinosaur fossil-bearing formation exposed in

North Dakota, marks the extinction of the last dinosaurs. The abundant dinosaur fossils in this formation include remains of *Triceratops, Torosaurus, Tyrannosaurus, Albertosaurus, Thescelosaurus, Pachycephalosaurus, Stygimoloch, Edmontosaurus, Troodon, Saurornitholestes,* and *Dromaeosaurus.* These were the last dinosaurs to ever live.

North Dakota is home of the "One that didn't get away." The mosasaur, a lizardlike animal that looked like a fish, grew to be up to forty-five feet long. Unlike its terrestrial lizard relatives, mosasaur limbs were modified flippers that helped the animal to steer underwater. Mosasaurs were active predators and among the main carnivores in the Western Interior Seaway. Although mosasaurs were not dinosaurs, they became extinct at the same time as the dinosaurs, about sixty-five million years ago.

The state fossil collection consists of some one hundred thousand individual specimens. This Web site allows you to search the database for fossil sites by county as well as view catalog entries on various specimens. Come here to learn more about North Dakota's dinosauria through photos of fossil recovery, educational activities, abstracts of research papers, and public digs.

Paso Partners—Integrating Mathematics, Science, and Language: A Bilingual Instructional Program
www.sedl.org/scimath/pasopartners/

Dinosaurs share the subject matter of this bilingual educational product called *Integrating Mathematics, Science and Language: A Bilingual Instructional Program,* a two-volume curriculum and resource guide. The resource is designed to help elementary school teachers organize their classrooms and instructional activities to increase achievement of Hispanic primary-grade children whose first language is not English. The guide offers a curriculum plan, instructional strategies and activities, suggested teacher and student materials, and assessment procedures. Accompanying each complete unit in English is a Spanish version of background information for the teacher as well as a Spanish version of the formal introductory portion of the lesson cycle.

This bilingual guide was developed by Paso Partners and involved three public schools, an institution of higher education, and specialists at the Southwest Educational Development Laboratory (SEDL). SEDL is a private, not-for-profit education research and development corporation based in Austin, Texas. Thirty years ago, SEDL began investigating early English language learning and developed curriculum materials for use in teaching English to Latino children.

The seven-lesson dinosaur unit is geared toward kindergartners and is available in both English and Spanish. You can access the entire module on-line, or as a fifty-nine-page downloadable PDF file. The guide includes a lesson overview, the "big ideas" of each lesson, background for teachers, and an objective grid. It is our opinion that the PDF version is much more desirable and easier to print out than the on-line version. To print out all of the pages, a teacher would have to click on every link to find them and hope that all pages have been found. While the PDF workbook is worthwhile (and free), the on-line version (also free) does not make full use of the Web as a medium.

Paul Sereno's Dinosaur Web Site

In 1988, Paul Sereno, a paleontology professor at the University of Chicago, was the famous paleontologist who discovered Jobaria of Africa, recently the subject of a *National Geographic Explorer* special. Paul Sereno also discovered the first complete skull and skeleton of the *Herrerasaurus* and four other partial skeletons in the Andes of Argentina. Together, these bones allowed a complete reconstruction of this early dinosaur now on display in the Field Museum of Natural History, Chicago.

Returning to Argentina in 1991, his team discovered a small, three-foot-long skeleton belonging to a new species. He named it the

Eoraptor (Dawn Raptor) for its commonality to all dinosaurs. Basing the age on nearby volcanic ash beds, the *Eoraptor* was estimated to be 228 million years old. These discoveries shed light on the roots of the dinosaur family tree and on how and when dinosaurs became the dominant animals on land. You can read all about his numerous discoveries on his artfully executed Web site.

To find dinosaurs, you have to go into the field and get them, no matter how remote or inhospitable. Many paleontologists rarely venture too far from home, motels, and fast food. This Web site takes you on snapshot adventures to Argentina, Niger, Morocco, and Patagonia. See for yourselves the rugged work of excavating in a sauropod graveyard.

Meet some of Dr. Sereno's discoveries on the Web site. *Afrovenator abakensis* (the Hunter from in [*sic*] Abaka, Africa) was found in Niger in 1993. This 130-million-year-old specimen is the most complete skeleton of a Cretaceous carnivore ever found in Africa. *Carcharodontosaurus saharicus* (Shark-toothed Reptile from the Sahara) was discovered on a 1995 Morocco expedition. Watch the *Discoveries Web Page* for a flesh reconstruction of *Suchomimus*, a predatory dinosaur discovered on the 1997 expedition to Niger.

Missing from this site is a button back to the home or index page. Without it, users might miss the interesting link (which only appears on the index page) to *Paul Sereno's Audio Discussion of the Science Article, Dinosaur Evolution* (dinosaur.uchicago.edu/continents/EvolutionFrame.html). Paul Sereno published his article "Dinosaur Evolution" in the June 25, 1999, issue of *Science*. The Web site includes separate sections on dinosaur radiation, the Dinosauria cladogram (treelike diagram showing evolutionary relationships), skeletal innovations among the major clades (classifications) of dinosaurs, the evolution of flight, and the evolutionary consequences of continental drift. There are two useful, screen-size charts of the dinosaur tree of life under the links *Evolving Over Time* and *Dinosauria*. In addition, he has posted two more charts explaining the dinosaur's *Skeletal Innovations* and the *Evolution of Flight*. The Web page features highlights from the article for general audiences. Listening to the audio requires a plug-in called QuickTime, version 3.0 or higher. If QuickTime is not on your computer, this Web site provides a link for downloading, but be aware that it takes about a half hour to an hour and a half to download.

The audio discussion of "Dinosaur Evolution" is the most fascinating piece on this Web site. Without it, though colorful and artistically done, Dr. Paul Sereno's Dinosaur Web Site is not a treasure trove of data. It does, however, offer an interesting insight into the career and lifestyle of an Indiana Jones–style paleontologist.

See also Project Exploration! at www.projectexploration.org, cofounded by Paul Sereno, about a dinosaur fossil lab and exhibits for children in the Chicago area. Visit Paul's other Web site about his famous African dinosaur, Jobaria, at: www.jobaria.org/.

Polyglot Paleontologist
www.uhmc.sunysb.edu/anatomicalsci/paleo/

Polyglot Paleontologist offers English translations of non-English paleontological literature—namely scientific papers on dinosaurs. (*Polyglot* means "speaking or writing in several languages.") Once a mostly European field, the science of vertebrate paleontology is now a worldwide discipline. Scientists from Argentina to Zimbabwe have contributed to the research in their native languages. Many of the first papers written about dinosaurs are still in French or German, and have not been translated into English, which is rising as the global language of science. Scientists over the years have labored to translate these papers, but without computers and copy machines, these translations were not available to everyone. Matthew Carrano created Polyglot Paleontologist as a place where scientists and laypeople can download existing translations, add their own translations to the database, and post requests for others. These papers range across all topics, time periods, and authors. Before using the database, however, researchers are asked to sign in, read the terms of use, and abide by them.

One of the earliest papers in the database is *"Premiere note sur les dinosaures de Bernissart,"* or "First note on the dinosaurs of Bernissart," by L. Dollo, published in *Bulletin du Musee Royale d'Histoire Naturelle de Belgique* in 1882. A more recent translation was of a 1997 Spanish paper, entitled "A new tetanuran (Dinosauria: Theropoda) from the Bajo Barreal Formation (Upper Cretaceous), Patagonia."

With nearly a hundred papers listed in the database, many of them translated by Matthew Carrano himself, this is an invaluable site for students who want to impress their teachers.

Vertebrate Phylogeny Pages
www.geocities.com/CapeCanaveral/Hall/1636/

"Dinosaurs may inspire years of schooling and careful thought about the fragile world and lead to interests in other vertebrates," writes Jack Conrad, author of the Vertebrate Phylogeny Pages. Vertebrates, via Dinosauria, have certainly become his passion. This page is meant to nurture the interest of children, serve as a reference for those looking for phylogenies of both extant and extinct vertebrates, and even serve to help experts as more complete bibliographies and links appear on the various Vertebrate Phylogeny Pages. The site includes a *Craniate Cladogram* and gives the option of using an *Express Page* to research specific clades. Groups include Craniata (vertebrates and their closest relatives), Gnathostomata (jawed vertebrates), Placodermi, Chondrichthyes, Actinopterygii ("ray-finned" fishes), Teleostei (advanced actinopterygians), Chondrostei, Sarcopterygia (vertebrates with "limbs"), Placodermi, Tetrapoda, Amniota (mammals, reptiles, and birds), Therapsida, Mammalia, Archosauriformes, Crocodylomorpha, and Dinosauria. See the author's sketches of skeletons and skulls on the *Bones* page, thoughtfully ordered for easy comparisons. This is a nicely organized, informative site for those interested in "branching out" from Dinosauria.

CHAPTER 3

DINO DEBATES

Debates About Dinosaurs
www.eleves.ens.fr:8080/home/ollivier/dinosaurs.html

Debates About Dinosaurs is not the home page of this site. That can be found at www.eleves.ens.fr:8080/home/ollivier/, simply called "Yann Ollivier." Besides paleontology, this site discusses mathematics (including a few articles he wrote mainly for *Quadrature* magazine), strange phenomena in the French language, philosophy, and music, some of which is in French only. The paleontology page is entirely in English. Topics in "Debates About Dinosaurs" include: metabolism, extinction, lifestyle, and the bird link. Under "metabolism," you'll find these problems: feathered dinosaurs, arctic and antarctic dinosaurs, predator/prey ratios, and posture and behavior. Under "extinction," subjects include iridium-bearing layer, shocked quartz, nickeliferous magnetites, various impact theories, the scheme of extinction, the marine regression hypothesis, and the volcanic hypothesis. Moving, running, feed, habitat, social structure, and intelligence are discussed under "lifestyles." Under the "dinosaur/bird link" Yann Ollivier explores *Archaeopteryx* and its links to both birds and dinosaurs, the "wishbone debate," feathers versus scales, the origin of flight, cursorial versus arboreal, and the relationships among early birds and birdlike dinosaurs. Obviously, this Web author is a broad thinker, and he has organized his site well. The debates are presented in succinct outline form, with little attention to artistic style.

Dinosaurs and the Expanding Earth
www.dinox.freeserve.co.uk/

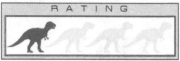

Dinosaurs and the Expanding Earth is a free on-line book (although the full book is available through amazon.co.uk for £40) that presents an explanation for the gigantic scale of prehistoric life. Studies indicate that dinosaurs were surprisingly more agile than they should have been, given their massive size in comparison to present-day life. A reduced gravity due possibly to a smaller earth during the dinosaurs' time might have allowed them to grow to gigantic sizes. Geological evidence suggests that the earth's diameter has increased since the dinosaurs' time. Outlandish? Perhaps. In the scientific world, such books on theories are read by a group of peer scientists. This book has not been "peer reviewed" but is nevertheless interesting.

The Web site briefly introduces some of the main concepts behind the theory. There are also links to other sites about gigantic dinosaurs and their lifestyles and the evidence for the expanding earth theory, a comments section, a quiz, and some suggestions for further reading.

Dinosaur Extinction: Volcano-Greenhouse
fbox.vt.edu:10021/artsci/geology/mclean/
Dinosaur_Volcano_Extinction/

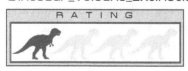

Sixty-five million years ago, some phenomenon triggered mass extinctions on the lands and in the oceans that were so profound, they define the geological boundary between the "Age of Reptiles" and the "Age of Mammals," or the Mesozoic and Cenozoic Eras. On a finer scale, the extinctions define the boundary between the Cretaceous ("K") and Tertiary ("T") Periods. The period in which the dinosaurs became extinct is therefore called the K-T extinction, and it is one of the great mysteries in science. Sea level change, supernova explosions, and climate change are just three of the early theories about what might have caused the K-T extinctions. Two new theories arose in the 1970s and 1980s and clashed in debate. One was the impact extinction (triggered by a giant asteroid) theory originated by the Nobel Prize–winning physicist Luis Alvarez and his team. The other, called "The K-T Deccan Traps Volcanism-Induced Carbon Cycle Pertubation Extinction Theory," was originated by Dewey McLean, the author of this Web site. He calls it the Volcano-Greenhouse Theory, for short. In other words: global warming.

The supporters of both theories clashed harshly in the great debate, with the impact theory becoming the favorite. The Web author regrets this, saying, "This conflict has been unfortunate for science because it prevented cooperation among scientists who were examining extinction processes via extraterrestrial mechanism and those who were examining them via earthly mechanisms." Why couldn't both theories work hand in hand?

McLean describes both theories in this scientific paper. What is fascinating about the article is watching the process of scientific scrutiny and politics. The paper includes links to relevant articles, references, a time line, and illustrations. This scientific paper illustrates why the World Wide Web was developed in the first place. A must for serious students.

End of a Legacy: How Did the Dinosaurs Meet Their Demise?

dinoextinction.homestead.com/files/

Approximately 230 million years ago, the first dinosaurlike lizard appeared. Within 5 million years that lizard evolved into what could truly be considered a dinosaur, rising to the top of the food chain. Then, 65 million years ago, the dinosaurs simply vanished. Perhaps the most unchallenged and powerful creatures on the earth at that time, or ever, had become extinct.

So begins the premise of this Web site, which explores various theories for the dinosaur disappearing act, including: "Death by Collision," "Recurring Mass Extinctions," "Global Temperature Changes," and "Death by Suffocation: The Pele Hypothesis." The page also includes endnotes and a bibliography. Although not extensive, this Web site (by eighth-grader Andrew Maas) is a good example to use in building one for a classroom project.

Evolution, Dinosaurs, Birds, Flightlessness, Archaeopteryx
www.geocities.com/CapeCanaveral/Hall/2099/DinoKabin.html

Johnny Jackson's home page (www.geocities.com/CapeCanaveral/Hall/2099/index.html) warns: "Viewers of a complacent disposition should be aware their minds may be changed!" This site, he claims, "reveals one of the most fascinating of the dinosaur theories of our time [linking to a glossary of theories about the bird-dinosaur link]; dissects the dubious 'science' lurking behind modern paleontology [linking to an essay on cladistics theory]; and considers the human weaknesses in scientific culture." The primary article, "The Bird-Dino Link," apparently focuses on the problems of cladistic theory.

Cladistic theory, he explains, starts with the "clade," a group of forms or creatures sharing a particular characteristic. All creatures sharing the feature "feathered," for instance, were placed in the "bird" clade. "Of course, this is the basic idea behind any reconstruction lines of evolution, but as usual, the devil lives in the details," he writes. Continuing, he says that if we were trying to fit a fossil animal with two toes into a line of prehistoric creatures with fewer toes over time, "most people could make a pretty good guess at where it should go!" But biology is full of reversals. Maybe toes don't increase in number (and maybe they do!) but other things definitely *do* go back. For example, whales went back to having flippers, after having proper legs. When fish first crawled out of the water, they had flipperlike structures.

Room 101, where you can interpret dinosaur/bird fossils, is just one of four rooms that can be explored in this Web site. Other subjects include artificial intelligence (*Room 102*), a book review of Terrence Deacon's *The Symbolic Species* (*Room 103*), and British fencing (*Room 104*).

This is an interesting read, and may be over the heads of younger children.

Kuban's K-Paleo Place: Fossils, Paleontology, Dinosaurs
members.aol.com/fostrak/kpaleo.htm
Secondary Site of Note:
Paluxy Dinosaur—"Man Track" Controversy
members.aol.com/paluxy2/paluxy.htm

Kuban's K-Paleo Place is the mother of all sites for links to Internet and Web resources on fossils, paleontology, natural history, and related topics, neatly and scientifically categorized with descriptions and comments for each link. Currently a programmer and systems analyst, Glen Kuban holds a degree in biology and a teacher's certificate (K–12), and is a member or officer of a number of paleontological societies, such as the Fossil Society of the Cleveland Museum of Natural History. His Web site has been the beneficiary of all these skills, interests, and education.

At Kuban's K-Paleo Place, users will find information on general paleontology, invertebrates, vertebrates, paleobotony, ichnology (tracks and other trace fossils), and geologic time. Interested in evolution or debates on creationism vs. Darwinism? Kuban's K-Paleo Place has the leads. Looking for natural history museums or university paleontology departments or paleontology publications? Come here. Teachers interested in educational sites or field trip planning, come here. You've come to the right place if you're a fossil enthusiast looking for other fossil enthusiasts, or for collection databases; commercial supplies, equipment, tours, and digs; or rock hound, mineral, and lapidary sites; or sites dealing with the legislation, rights, and ethics of collecting. How about mailing lists, societies, clubs, newsgroups, or professional geological resources? You'll find them all right here. What if you're tired of it all and just want a few laughs? Well, Kuban's K-Paleo Place might have a link just for you.

It's important to keep a sense of humor, for Kuban's other Web site deals with the creationism-Darwinism controversy. Most notably, the Paluxy "man track" controversy is the backbone of his interests. Kuban began his research on the Paluxy "man track" controversy in 1980 and formally presented his findings to the First International Symposium on Dinosaur Tracks and Traces in Albuquerque, New Mexico. These papers were included in the book *Dinosaur Tracks and Traces,* published in 1989 by Cambridge University Press. Kuban believes his Paluxy work helped prompt many "creationists to largely abandon the 'man track' claims," although his intent was not to attack creationism or Christianity, being a Christian himself, but to help set the record straight on the true nature of the Paluxy evidence.

What is the Paluxy controversy? For many years people believed that a giant man left his footprints alongside the tracks of a dinosaur in the limestone beds of the Paluxy River near Glen Rose, Texas. If true, such a find would have dramatically contradicted the conventional geologic timetable, which put the appearance of humans on earth at least sixty million years after the disappearance of dinosaurs. These tracks were most likely the tail impressions, foot slides, and toe draggings of a bipedal dinosaur, eroded, discolored, and tampered with over time. On his site, Kuban has placed more than a one hundred printed pages of articles, written largely by him.

Although visually uninteresting, Kuban's K-Paleo Place and the adjoining Paluxy Dinosaur/"Man Track" Controversy, is a wealth of information by a prolific Web author, presented in a clear, scientific order.

The Talk.Origins Archive
www.talkorigins.org/

Talk.origins is a Usenet newsgroup devoted to the discussion and debate of biological and physical origins. Most discussions in the newsgroup center on the creation-evolution controversy, but other topics of discussion include the origin of life, geology, biology, catastrophism, cosmology, and theology.

The Talk.Origins Archive is a collection of articles and essays that explore the creationism-evolution controversy from a mainstream scientific perspective. In other words, the authors of most of the articles in this archive accept the prevailing scientific view that the earth is ancient, that there was no global flood, and that evolution is responsible for the earth's present biodiversity.

The archive was established in 1994 to provide easy access to the many FAQ (frequently asked question) files and essays that were being posted regularly to the Usenet newsgroup Talk.origins. Since that time, the archive has grown immensely. It now houses a *post of the month* feature, a local search engine, a user feedback page, and an extensive list of links to other Web sites dealing with the creation-evolution controversy.

The archive's policy is that readers should be given easy access to alternative views, but those who espouse alternative views should speak for themselves. Hence, the archive supplies links to relevant creationist Web sites within many of its articles. It also maintains a frequently updated and extensive *list of creationist and catastrophist Web sites* so that readers may familiarize themselves with antievolutionary perspectives on scientific issues.

Talk.origins readers participate in Usenet discussions by reading and "posting" articles with special news-reading software. Examples of popular news-reading software for Windows and Macintosh platforms include Netscape Navigator news reader, Microsoft Internet Explorer news reader, and Forte Free Agent. The articles that are posted in the Talk.origin archives are readable in any HTML browsers, such as Netscape and Explorer.

Before posting to Talk.origins, you are strongly encouraged to review the Talk.Origins Welcome FAQs and the Talk.Origins Archive FAQs. If you post to Talk.origins with a question or challenge that has already been answered by one of the many FAQs, you will probably be met with scorn.

Although it isn't clear who sponsors the Talk.Origins Archive or newsgroup, a link to *University of Ediacara* is prominently posted on the index page. The university (U of E) is an on-line virtual university dedicated to the study of the origins of life in the cosmos.

CHAPTER 4

JUNIOR PALEONTOLOGISTS

Dino Land Web Site
www.geocities.com/CapeCanaveral/Galaxy/8152/
Steve Brusatte, Canada, Age 16

At first glance, it would appear that there is not much to this site, but what it lacks in design and speed it gains in ambition. The large title links on the contents page do not do justice to the site's vastness, and there is no complete map or mode of navigation. But if you hunt around a little by following all of the links, you will find a wealth of material.

Before going beyond the index page, take note of the link called *This Just In*. Here readers can discover the very latest dinosaur news. Links lead to Web reprints of the original articles. The Brusatte brothers (Steve and Chris) stay current with the news.

Click on the *Carcharodontosaurus* tooth to enter Dino Land and meet paleontologists. What distinguishes the official Dino Land site from others are the exclusive interviews with "some of your favorite paleontologists." These include Robert Bakker (who "needs no introduction"), Peter Dodson (who discovered the *Avaceratops* in 1986), Peter Sheehan (who led a study that showed dinos died out quickly), Michael Brett-Surman (Smithsonian paleontologist), Cathy Forster (major backer of dinosaur-bird evolution), Mike Everhart (discovered a new mosasaur and discusses the truth of the Loch Ness Monster myth), and James Farlow (Indiana paleontologist who studies dino-motion). Continue scrolling through the contents page for more links to interviews. Dino Land conducted some ninety interviews of famous paleontologists for a future book. (The site includes contact, E-mail, and Web site information for these paleontologists.) Apparently, according to the Web authors, no one has previously undertaken a project of this magnitude.

Continue scrolling down for the latest news in dinosaur science, or to links to a feature called "Travels in Paleontology." Springboard into the *Dinosaurs 2000* Web site about dinosaur finds on the cusp of the millennium. Or join the Dino Land Dinosaur Dig Club sponsored by Yahoo! at: clubs.yahoo.com/clubs/thedinolanddinosaur digsite. Or go to a current issue of the *Dino Land Dinosaur Gazette,* a meaty E-zine, edited by Steve Brusatte, that is open to subscriptions by E-mail.

But wait! Dino Land offers French, Dutch, Swedish, and Portuguese versions of the site. A Web page called *Dinosaurs International,* within the official Dino Land site, offers articles in these languages plus Italian, Nederlandse, and soon, Spanish, Polish, and Norske.

Dino Land is devoted to paleontology, especially amateur collecting and writing. Readers may be surprised to learn that Steve Brusatte, a sixteen-year-old sophomore at Ottawa High School, is the project's author. Chris Brusatte, an eleven-year-old sixth grader at Wallace Grade School, plans to help by illustrating. Steve Brusatte has written more than twenty articles appearing in various magazines and journals, including *Fossil News, Dinosaur World,* and the *Prehistoric Times.* According to Chris Brusatte's biography, he founded Dino Land museum in the corner of his bedroom in 1991. He was only three years old at the time. Chris hired his brother Steve to become curator of geology.

Do not be deceived by the youthfulness of the Web authors or their tongue-in-cheek sense of humor. These are bright young men, and their information appears to be reliable.

Dinosaur Cladograms
by Øyvind Mario Padron
home.sol.no/~enrique
by Øyvind Mario Padron, Trødelag, Norway, Age 18

Øyvind Mario Padron (his friends call him Gorgosaur) is an eighteen-year-old artist from Norway. He has applied his talent to dozens of neatly and expertly drawn illustrations, all carefully displayed with explanations for choosing certain characteristics. He takes you through the steps he takes to draw dinosaurs. First he chooses an "enigmatic" subject, like an *Erlikosaurus,* usually connected to a theory of his. Then he scans through books and sketches, although it is difficult to get good material, he says. He turns to the Internet, books, museum and university collections, and paleontological journals, in search of actual photographs of bones. He prefers photographs over artist renderings, because artists tend to repair fractures and fill in the missing pieces. That's the part he seems to enjoy doing himself. For an *Erliksaurus,* he might find a skull minus a lower jaw and so fills that in with the lower jaw of a *Segnosaurus.* Sometimes he has to rely on a reconstruction. Once he sketches out the bone structure, he imagines the muscles, skin, lips, eyes, nasal openings, scales, and so on.

Øyvind doesn't just draw, he muses. In *DinoMix,* he says: "Everybody knows about the golfball-sized brain the stegosaurs carried, but has anybody realized that the stegosaurids were smarter than, say, a shark? Make a list of every animal the stegosaurs were smarter than, and you'll change your view." This is an example of what some eighteen-year-old dinosaur artists think about.

This Web site includes dinosaur cladograms, a time line, news, history, dinosaur book reviews, notes on dinosaur extinction, some frequently asked questions, some photographs of skeletons, a list of errors he found in *Jurassic Park,* the movie, and dinosaurs in Norway, a subject he is particularly enthusiastic about.

Øyvind's broken English is understandable, but his pages are full of misspellings. Overlooking that, this is a pleasant site to visit.

Grant Harding's Dinosaur Destination
www.cyberus.ca/~sharding/grant/
by Grant Harding, High School Student

Grant Harding, a high school student from Ottawa, Canada, asks these questions: Which came first, the chicken or the egg? Did dinosaurs have feathers? The answer to the first question, supported by an essay he wrote and published on his Web site, is that birds came first. That is, maybe there were birds before there were dinosaurs. The answer to the second question, discussed in another essay, is that fossils show some dinosaurs may have had "proto-feathers."

Grant is re-creating a dinosaur ecosystem using SimLife, a program that allows the user to create animals and plants, then set them loose in a virtual world. He chose the Judith River Formation because his favorite dinosaur, *Troodon,* was discovered there. The Judith River Formation has since been split into many formations. He is now focusing on the Dinosaur Park Formation, which is one of only two places in the world in which a true dinosaur ecosystem can be read in the rocks (the second being the Nemegt Valley in Mongolia). The project, though, still bears the unofficial name of Judith River. Stay tuned to this page for developments on his ecosystem.

Jennifer's Dinosaurs
www.geocities.com/EnchantedForest/Cottage/3216/
by Jennifer, Age 6

Jennifer loves *T. rexes,* and she loves collecting all sorts of bright, colorful cartoons and animation of dinosaurs. "Fun Stuff" provides links to dinosaur puzzles, games, songs, origami, kites, on-line adventures, crafts, pictures, and stories. A cute site for kids and well organized, although downloading all of the pieces does seem never-ending.

Jonathan's Utahraptor Page
www.kiva.net/~penguin/utahrapt.html
by Jonathan Craton, Age 12

The *Utahraptor* (Utah hunter) was discovered by Dr. Jim Kirkland in a desert near Moab, Utah, in 1991, at about the same time the movie *Jurassic Park* hit theaters. The dinosaur's more formal name is *Utahraptor ostrommaysi*, the latter named after John Ostrom, a scientist, and Chris Mays, the founder of a robotics firm called Dinamation International. This twenty-foot, half-ton carnivore with razor-sharp claws lived during the Late Early Cretaceous Period 125 million years ago. You can read all about the *Utahraptor* at this Web site.

Opus: Web Pages
members.gotnet.net/maier/
by Daniel Bensen, Age 16

Opus means "foot" in Latin, and a dinosaur name based on footprints will have the suffix at the end of the generic (first) name. More then a mere Web site, Opus: Web Pages is a whimsical electronic scrapbook with odds and ends and drawings about dinosaurs, aliens, and other living animals—but mostly dinosaurs. Daniel Bensen presents his Web site like a field notebook, as if he coexisted with the dinosaurs and observed them while in the field. In *Opus: Dinosaurs*, each dinosaur classification includes a drawing (we can assume that he drew most of them) and a description. He provides links to the Web sites of experts for timely information. Particularly amusing is Dan Bensen's on-line journal. In *Talkabout*, he gives an overview of the site. Scroll to the bottom for new, dated entries, and an autobiography. Look for the link to *Thoughts*, an amusing self-portrait drawing, called "Athor's Ravinge," purposely misspelled, and a sixteen-week journal, which actually begins at the bottom of the

Web page, with the final sixteenth-week entry at the top. Here is an excerpt from Week Six of his journal:

> I have added all the species of true Mesozoic birds (with the exception of four which are proving difficult to draw) that I was able to find onto "OPUS: Dinosaur." The problem, I find, with reconstructing birds from skeletons is that the skeletons give the false impression of belonging to long-necked, small-headed, short-shinned animals completely different from what the real thing looked like.

Daniel has lived on both coasts in his short sixteen years of life, but perhaps his most interesting time was when he lived at the University of Chicago in a dorm where his parents were resident heads. "I have no idea how much the experience of living with twenty or more college students warped me," he writes. This Web site, though the obvious work of a teenager, exhibits a unique blend of talent, scientific interest and approach, and a vivid imagination.

CHAPTER 5

FOSSILS AND FIELD TRIPS

Dinosaur Tracking Field Trips
www.neosoft.com/~medmunds/

The family that tracks together, stays together. The Edmundses go dino tracking on their vacations, and you can follow in their footsteps on their Web site, where they've posted an overview of several trips, complete with photographs, maps, itineraries, specific driving instructions, and a reading list for each site.

In October 1995, Mike, his wife Debbie, and son Sean visited the Lower Cretaceous Dinosaur Trackways in central Texas. These included the well-preserved sauropod trackway in the Blanco River bed outside the town of Blanco and the theropod prints in Austin's Zilker Park and the South Fork valley of the San Gabriel River trackway north of Leander. The recipe they used for casting theropod prints with dental alginate Jeltate is included in this section. In 1998 they returned to the Blanco River sauropod track site to measure any damage that might have occurred during a particularly tropical rain season. In 1996 they visited Jurassic dinosaur trackways in Picket Wire Canyon in southeastern Colorado, reputedly the largest dinosaur trackway in North America. Here the authors give hiking and safety tips for hiking to these tracks. The year 1997 found the Edmunds family on Navajo and Hopi tribal lands near Tuba City, Arizona, tracking Jurassic-age *Dilophosauripus williamsi, Kayentapus hoppi,* and *Hopiiichnus shingii,* all theropods. (Please seek permission from tribal offices before looking for dinosaur tracks on reservations. These sites are often considered sacred.)

As an added bonus, the Edmundses have included an extensive page for *Casting Dinosaur Footprints.* The page lists step-by-step instructions and photographs. This is a good site for families interested in a different kind of outing or for school groups living in the Four Corners area of the United States.

The Prehistoric Times
www.gremlins.com/prehistoric_times/

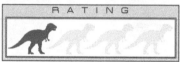

Rather than provide information about dinosaurs, this site provides information about the *Prehistoric Times,* a bimonthly, forty-page print magazine for the dinosaur model collector and enthusiast. Each issue has a full-color cover and contains reviews of model kits, modeling tips, histories of dino models, toys and sculptures, interviews with people involved in the dinosaur world today, and much more. The magazine subscription is not free, but trial and back issues are available for seven dollars. The contents of each issue are described when clicking on the thumbnail picture of a particular cover, which appears on the index page.

Skullduggery—Fossil Replicas and Science Kits
www.skullduggery.com

Throughout the past decade and a half, there has been a huge increase in fossil interest from the general public. Professionals and well-trained amateurs can learn a great deal from studying fossils and the sites from which they are found. Unfortunately, the selling of real fossil material to the highest bidder has created an atmosphere for the destruction of valuable scientific data. Many untrained fossil hunters, who hunt for profit, risk the destruction of an important discovery in order to find valuable fossils to be sold on the open market. Once the fossils are sold to individual collectors, they are out of the reach and view of the general public. They are no longer available for exhibit in museums.

Established in 1978, it has been Skullduggery's longstanding policy never to sell original fossil material. With Skullduggery, a collector can own a fossil replica that is identical to the original. The real fossils remain safely housed in museums throughout the world to be seen and studied by anyone. Skullduggery pays royalties to these museums for every cast sold.

They create a detailed mold from the original specimen and then hand-cast a full-size replica. The proprietary molding and casting process duplicates the intricate details of the original with accuracy; the sutures, muscle origins, and fine cranial pitting are clearly visible. Each cast is then hand-polished with a tar pit or antique finish to create the most authentic fossil replica possible.

Skullduggery sells a replica of a *Tyrannosaurus rex* tooth and claw on display at the Museum of Geology in South Dakota, and *Utahraptor* and *Deinonychus* claws housed at the Peabody Museum of Natural History at Yale University and the College of Eastern Utah Prehistoric Museum, respectively. The six-inch-by-six-inch-by-two-and-a-half-inch hadrosaur egg that Skullduggery has replicated is the largest and most complete ever discovered. Skullduggery has also replicated an *Oviraptor* egg, six inches by two and a half inches, containing an almost complete skeleton of an *Oviraptor* embryo. Check out the foot-long *Allosaurus* embedded in rock. Skullduggery also offers replicas of two *Tyrannosaurus* skulls and a *Triceratops* skull. In addition to fossils, Skullduggery fashions exquisite steel *Tyrannosaurus* and *Velociraptor* skeletons.

Skullduggery fossil replicas are used for study in major colleges and universities, displayed in museums throughout the world, and collected by people with a love of natural history. Educational booklets are provided for most of the replicas.

Skullduggery has developed hands-on Classroom Kits, MuseumWorks Kits, and Eyewitness Science Kits designed specifically for direct student participation. Classroom Kits are designed for up to six students ages eight and up. Within this category, two Fossil Kits take students on an interactive journey into the fascinating world of fossil exploration and identification. One kit includes a dinosaur claw while the other packs a dino egg. Fossilworks fosters awareness and appreciation of the earth's history by casting and finishing replicas of a dinosaur claw, among other pieces. Dino Traces takes students on a realistic dinosaur excavation simulation by making rubbings of a *Triceratops, Tyrannosaurus,* or *Velociraptor,* assembling their skeletons, and discussing the way paleontologists would approach a dinosaur dig and subsequent discovery.

Eyewitness Kits are also designed for individual students ages eight and up. With each Eyewitness Kit students can read along in the illustrated educational booklets and learn as they study dinosaur skeletal systems, internal organs, living environments of extinct animals, and more as they cast, paint, and proudly display their work. In one of three Dinoworks Kits, students can cast and paint eighteen to nineteen bone structures to assemble and display a nineteen-inch *Tyrannosaurus* skeleton, a fifteen-inch *Triceratops* skeleton, or a twenty-four-inch *Velociraptor* skeleton. In MuseumWorks Kits, individual students age eight and up can remove the seam line and finish an eleven-inch *T. rex* tooth or a seven-inch *Utahraptor* claw for display. Lesson plans for all of these kits are downloadable for free in PDF on the Web site.

This is a multifaceted site. Skullduggery offers nondinosaur fossil and skull replicas, so be sure to use the site's search engine to discover all of the dinosaur material.

Smith Studios Discovery Kits: The Best Way to Discover Dinosaurs!
www.discoverykit.com/

Smith Studios offers two Discovery Kits that promise to be "an educational adventure for the amateur paleontologist." With Discovery Kits you can dig or cast your very own dinosaur fossil reproduction. The fossils and casts are reproductions of actual fossils on display in museums in the United States and around the world.

One Discovery Kit is the Excavation Kit. Paleontologists often encase dinosaur fossils in plaster jackets for protection and then dig out the fossil when back in the laboratory. Excavation Kits provide the actual experience of digging an authentic fossil reproduction cast in a plaster-jacketed dirtlike substance. The kits also include the necessary digging tools, a brush, a field map, and directions.

The other Discovery Kit product is a Casting Kit. Since dinosaur fossils are valuable, paleontologists often study authentic reproductions. Casting Kits provide real-life experiences in making casts of an actual fossil. Each Casting Kit includes a museum-quality silicone mold made from an actual dinosaur fossil. Also included are three bags of plaster, three mixing bowls, a mixing spoon, and a field map.

Both kits contain photographs and scientifically accurate, easy-to-read information that explains how fossils are excavated and how authentic casts are made. Also included is information about the dinosaur and the fossil reproduction contained in the kit. The materials, tools, and activities simulate the actual equipment and techniques used by real paleontologists.

Discovery Kits also aid research in paleontology around the world. A royalty on every reproduction is paid to the institution that holds the original fossil. This income helps fund research and assists in the preservation of fossils.

Timescale Adventures
timescale.3rivers.net/

Timescale Adventures is located in the Bynum-Choteau area of Montana, along the Rocky Mountain front, halfway between Great Falls and Glacier National Park on Highway 89. This area is noted worldwide for its spectacular paleontological discoveries, geological exposures, wildlife habitat, and Native American historical and archaeological sites. Timescale Adventures chose this impressive area to provide hands-on programs for the general public. Conducted at active research sites, professional researchers and instructors provide informative and entertaining experiences for all ages and interests. Staff members have been conducting public field programs in this area since 1968.

Timescale offers three-hour seminars teaching basic fossil recognition, history, and geology on-site. A three-hour Campfire Paleontology Session includes discussions by the paleontologist and historian, music, stories, songs, and a barbecue. One-day seminars cover information on paleontology and geology in the area, combined with digging at an active site. Add a second day for an extended experience in field collecting and fossil preservation. Ten-day sessions go in-depth into all aspects of field paleontology, including discovery, collection, preservation, and interpretation, focusing on discoveries in the Two Medicine Formation. This program is also available for teacher recertification credits. Groups or individuals can order customized seminars to study particular topics suited to specific interests. The staff is experienced in most areas of biology, geology, archaeology, history, and Native American studies.

Beginning with the Fall 1999 issue, Timescale publishes an on-line newsletter about its activities, such as the building of its research facility, its publications and presentations, the setting up of a reconstruction of *Seismosaurus halli*, meetings, discoveries, staff members, affiliate paleontologists, and future plans.

Web readers can take a virtual field trip on this site. The premise: You've completed your research, and you've got your permits and permissions. It all seemed so easy on paper, but now you're faced with the reality of it. The prairie is wide, and the "treasure" you seek is so small. Where do you start? What do you look for? See what you find by following the links on the site.

Parts of this site were still under construction when we visited. Timescale plans to post the latest news, press releases, and a bulletin board for submitted exhibit information. Another planned Web page is a virtual on-line museum of important Late Cretaceous specimens from Montana found by Timescale digs. This is envisioned as part of a fossil registry program, whereby specimens found by various programs and individuals will be cataloged, described, and displayed in this virtual museum. Then researchers wanting to find out about what is out there for particular species can research and view specimens on-line and can also make arrangements to view and study the specimens directly wherever they reside.

Two Guys Fossils
www.twoguysfossils.com/

Specializing in all varieties of dinosaur fossils, Two Guys Fossils is a top supplier of museum-quality fossils, reproductions, posters, and dinosaur models at reasonable prices. If it's not in stock, Two Guys can usually locate most unusual specimens and will ship anywhere on the planet. That's good because customers come from the four corners of the world: Ripley's Believe It or Not!; Philadelphia Academy of Sciences; Yale-Peabody Museum; Pacific Science Center-Seattle; Carnegie Museum; New Orleans Geological Society; Weinman Mineral Museum, Georgia; Buffalo Museum of Science, New York; Disney Studios; Toyama Medical and Pharmaceutical University, Japan; and the Lunar and Planetary Labs at the University of Arizona, to name just a few.

Most of the fossils are shown on the Web site and can be ordered on-line, although it is recommended to order the catalog. Besides dinosaur items such as skulls, bones, teeth, eggs, and fossils, Two Guys also sells dinosaur models and a large range of posters. They make holiday gift-giving, beginner's, and decorator suggestions too. They keep an updated file on fossil news, including the latest arrest for the criminal collection of fossils, and there is an extensive list of related links here.

As if this weren't enough, Two Guys also sells an educational curriculum, called "Digging into the Past," designed to inspire and excite students in the study of dinosaurs. Using actual fossil materials and the latest information, students understand how dinosaurs lived millions of years ago. It not only adds new dimensions to the classroom with practical hands-on experience but also gives the students a working knowledge of the science of paleontology. It has been expressly developed to meet the new National Standards for Earth Science. The curriculum includes: The Life of a Dinosaur, The Dinosaur Egg, The Dinosaur Nest, Dinosaurs Grow Up, Putting Dinosaurs Back Together, Is It Bone or Stone? The Great Dinosaur Puzzle, Where Did Dinosaurs Go? Dinosaur Decorations, and In the Mouth of a Dinosaur. This is not an on-line curriculum;

student and teacher written materials, in addition to the purchase of fossils, are required.

Navigating Two Guy Fossils is as fun, interesting, and easy as turning the pages of a catalog.

Western Paleontological Laboratories, Inc.
www.itsnet.com/~western/wplhome.html

Not all jobs in paleontology are connected with museums or universities. Here's a company that excavates and restores dinosaur skeletons for profit. Western Paleontological Laboratories, Inc., is one of the largest and most experienced private fossil laboratories in the world, with exhibits in the United States, Europe, and Asia. Much of the material that WPL prepares comes from its own Jurassic quarries, and the company collects it in a scientific manner, precisely documenting each step of the excavation so that study can continue on the find by academics. The lab builds exhibits for museums, supplies quality fossils, insects, shells, and other natural history specimens, makes mold materials (e.g., latex, silicone), and produces casts in several different types of resins. Samples of their work can be viewed on this Web site. Museums and other scientific groups are invited to collect from WPL's Jurassic quarries.

Not long ago, during a field season at one of their Wyoming quarries, WPL discovered the partial skeleton of an unusual dinosaur lying very close to the surface. Fortunately, enough of the specimen still existed to identify it as a new Jurassic ankylosaur. The lab donated this unique skeleton to the Denver Museum of Natural History.

Forces of nature are steadily degrading the quality of dinosaur bones near the surface of the ground. Wind, rain, snow, and freeze-thaw cycles wear down and shatter this fragile record of the past. Some of the skeletons WPL finds are purchased by private individuals interested in saving the dinosaur for scientific posterity. The dinosaurs are then put on display in museums.

CHAPTER 6

DINO ART

A to Z One-at-a-Time List of Dinosaurs
web.syr.edu/~dbgoldma/pictures.html

So many great illustrations of dinosaurs exist on the Internet that it is difficult to hunt them all down. A to Z One-at-a-Time List of Dinosaurs offers a shortcut to the specific dinosaur you're looking for. Click on one of more than a hundred dinosaur names in alphabetical order on the main page, and you will be given a single thumbnail-size picture, along with the artist's name and its original site. Click on the thumbnail, and you'll be taken directly to the location of the dinosaur picture within that dinosaur's original site, whether it be *National Geographic* or the Peabody Museum. You can also navigate through the icon pages, which display about thirty-five small GIFs per page. These pages may take a little while to load, depending on Internet traffic at a given time. The *Panorama* link presents a handful of beautiful murals that also exist on the Web.

Another great feature of this site is the ability to send dino post cards to your friends. Choose one of eight dinosaur illustrations, fill in your own words, and E-mail to the lucky recipient. (You can use HTML code to format your message.) In a couple of days, you will receive an E-mail message saying your post card was received. It really works.

An ongoing, invaluable resource.

Dinosaur Art and Modeling
www.indyrad.iupui.edu/public/jrafert/dinoart.html

Don't judge this Web site by its home page. The Web author doesn't introduce the purpose of his site—but that's okay. Once you start clicking on the links in the left-frame menu, you'll soon see that this is the granddaddy of directories to dinosaur art and modeling on the Web. More than just a gateway to other Web sites, this site provides at least one page about the artist and sample artwork. When you follow a link to the artist's own home page, you actually go to a copy built right into John Rafert's site. This makes it difficult to bookmark the original home page or to see any updates the artist might have made, but you won't have to worry about chasing down dead links in cases where the artist has changed servers.

What's new on Dinosaur Art and Modeling? Apparently lots. You'll find more information on dino art and models on the *What's New?* page than on the *Artists* page. Much information was added to the site in 1999. The new *Readers Art* page publishes dinosaur work that has been sent to John Rafert. You can also read reviews of dinosaur modeling *kits* as well as kits that are specifically designed for *Tyrannosaurus* lovers.

John Rafert is a paleoartist himself, although he won't readily admit this. A link to one of his drawings occasionally pops up in different menus.

Dinosaur Art and Modeling is easy to navigate, downloads quickly, and is a precious resource.

The Dinosaur Art of Joe Tucciarone
members.aol.com/Dinoplanet/joe.html

Joe Tucciarone is a world-famous artist, whose subjects range from distant galaxies to the long-vanished dinosaurs. Visit one of his prehistoric animal galleries, where you'll see *Meat-Eating Reptiles, Plant-Eating Reptiles,* and *Ancient Mammals.* Many of these paintings are part of "Masters of the Earth," a traveling exhibit featuring the best of Tucciarone's dinosaur art. His astronomical images can be found on this site by clicking on the asteroid.

Joe's dinosaur illustrations have been published in magazines such as *Science* and *Discover.* His "Extinction" image appeared in the movie *Deep Impact* and the TBS *Fire from the Sky* television documentary. Joe's astronomical artwork has been commissioned several times by *National Geographic* magazine, and his space art has often appeared in *Sky and Telescope, Astronomy,* and *The Planetary Report* magazines. He recently brought together two of his childhood interests by writing and illustrating a planetarium show about dinosaurs. Novagraphics Space Art Gallery, the world's largest distributor of space-art laser lithographs, carries Joe's limited-edition prints and original space-art paintings.

Dinosaur Art/Paleo Art
by John Bindon
www.bindonillustrations.on.ca/

John Bindon displays ten scans of dinosaur paintings on his elegant Web site. With titles like *Terror at Dawn, No Escape,* and *Storm Front,* these watercolors and acrylics are action packed. John is a professional paleoartist, having designed three murals for the Lost World Touring Exhibit and colorations of a life-size robotic dinosaur currently in production. He has done character devel-

opment designs for Disney's *Dinosaur* and background paintings
for Discovery Television's *Giganotosaurus* animation sequences.
Worth checking out, but there's not a wealth of information.

Dinosaur Man!
www.dinosaur-man.com/dino.html

This is a straightforward Web site about a man and his dinosaur—
dinosaur art, that is. Images by Dinosaur Man, aka Rich Penney,
have been used to illustrate breaking science news stories by the
BBC, *CBS Evening News, Good Morning America, Dateline,* The
Learning Channel, *Natural History* magazine, *Scientific American,
Science News,* and *Earth* magazine. The images have also been pub-
lished in a number of national science magazines. A resident of
New Mexico, Penney's work is used by the New Mexico Natural
History Museum.

Penney paints in an academically classical style. After thirty-
five years of honing his skills with portraiture, wildlife, and landscapes, this traditional oil painter now specializes exclusively in
paleoart. He starts with the fossil record, applies his knowledge
of animal anatomy and comparative biology, and consults with
professional paleontologists for technical assistance. A master of
this rare forensic craft, he painstakingly reconstructs creatures that
have not walked the earth in more than sixty-five million years.

One-time rights are available for purchase, or Penney may be
commissioned to create original murals, oil paintings, or sketches.
Most of the Dinosaur Man paintings in this Web gallery are available for purchase, as well as prints, a poster, T-shirts, and slides
for educational presentations.

Dinosaurs "Dinotreker"
(Dinosaur Habitat Dioramas and Paleo Art)
www.dinotreker.com

Within this site you will find a unique and interesting view of dinosaurs. Unlike most dinosaur Web sites, you won't see scale models of dinosaurs mounted on a piece of stained wood or sculpted in bronze or paintings or drawings depicting them in a two-dimensional world. Here you will journey back seven million years and see dinosaurs living in their own lifelike three-dimensional habitat. Actually see the dinosaurs interacting with each other and the paleoworld around them: the *Triceratops* sampling the low-growing foliage, the *Velociraptor* quenching his thirst at the lakeside, or the surprise attack of the *Tyrannosaurus rex.*

The artist, Michael Rusher, was a landscaper for more than twenty years, which gave him an abundance of knowledge on plants, plant growth, and landscapes. His knowledge of the outdoors has enabled him to re-create the most realistic plant life and landscapes in miniature that will take you a step farther into the world of the dinosaur.

Some of the products sold through this site include a large photo print of a diorama, a "2000 Dino Data" calendar, diorama screensavers, T-shirts, mouse pads, wall clocks, coffee mugs, place mats, post cards, and bookmarks. Join the Dinosaur Mailing List and receive *The Dino-Source Newsletter,* a monthly publication full of dinosaur news from around the world.

Lost Worlds—The Paleolife Art of Brian Franczak
www.geocities.com/CapeCanaveral/Launchpad/2045/

A native of Connecticut, Brian Franczak found himself inspired to paint dinosaurs when he moved to the semitropical landscape of Florida at age twenty-four. Since the first publication of his work in 1989, he has become one of the world's leading paleolife illustrators. Brian Franczak has produced well over five hundred illustrations of dinosaurs.

His credits include such books as *The Complete T. rex* by John R. Horner and Don Lessem, the gift edition of Michael Crichton's *Jurassic Park*, the *Dinosaur Society Dinosaur Encyclopedia*, and The *Audubon Society Pocket Guide to Familiar Dinosaurs*. His work has also appeared in *Time, Omni,* and *Discover* magazines, the technical journals *National Geographic Research* and *Modern Geology*, and the television series *Nova* on PBS and *Paleoworld* on The Learning Channel. Calendars, post cards, trading cards, and CD-ROMs have also featured his illustrations. He is a long-standing member of the Society of Vertebrate Paleontology and consults with dinosaur paleontologists and fellow dinosaur illustrators.

More than merely viewing sample artwork of some famous artist, this is a chance to peer over the artist's shoulder as he draws, watching as his imagination turns white space into a character from the dawn of time. Judging from his Web site, Brian's imagination is vivid, extensive, and generous. All pages include introductions and notes that describe why he chose to illustrate the subject.

What's New offers current additions and changes to this site. *Introduction* answers the question "Why Dinosaurs?" and posts a cover gallery of the books he read as a kid. *Ceratopsians* showcases those Mesozoic marvels, the horned dinosaurs. Color profiles and "infobits" about predatory dinosaurs are included in the *Theropod Gallery. Tyrannosaurus Rex!* is a collection of illustrations of his favorite predatory dinosaur. In *Paintings* and *Archives* there are some obscure published pieces and details from recent, mostly unpublished paintings in his "Portraits" series. *Sketchbook* is a collection of studies, concept drawings, and pose sketches for paintings. *Argentina Sketchbook* features on-the-spot sketches of some of Argentina's mounted dinosaur skeletons and other related fossils. *Newly Discovered Dinosaurs* is devoted to illustrating these finds (with some slightly more familiar animals from the last decade or so thrown in to fill the spaces). Every good dinosaur illustration starts with an accurate skeletal drawing, and a few Brian has drawn over the years are exhibited in *Skeletal Drawings*. In *Other Mesozoic Denizens* we are reminded that not all extinct animals were dinosaurs, and that not all paleolife art must feature dinosaurs. This covers the highlights.

Brian's enthusiasm for his work is evident in his Web site. He writes: "By presenting new dinosaur discoveries with scientifically accurate artwork of both the animal and its environment, as well as up-to-date information about the animal, its relationships, and its discoverer(s), it is my hope that the dinosaur-loving public will get the sense that dinosaur paleontology is a living, growing science, with many exciting discoveries still to be made—maybe even by someone reading these words."

USA Dinosaur Pictures
www.sandsculpture.com/dino1.htm

A showcase for the United Sculptors of America (USA), this site is only partially about dinosaurs, but we wanted you to see it anyway. Twelve photographs of dinosaur sand sculptures are displayed here, and they're glorious. See *T. rex* and *Triceratops* fighting one another in shopping malls, or a baby dinosaur hatching from a gigantic egg. The medium of grains of sand lends itself to detail, no doubt, to the credit of the sculptors.

The Worlds of Mike Keesey
dinosaur.umbc.edu/keesey

This home page opens to a snapshot of a virtual galaxy—Mike Keesey–style. Click on *Saturn* to go to the Dinosauricon. If you're looking for information, you'll find it in the *Genus Index,* featuring an alphabetical list of all dinosaurs (except for neornithean birds), plus relatives like pterosaurs and lagosuchians; or in *Classification,* which gives all groups, plus a master cladogram. *Search Forms* yields various methods of sorting through the data. You can search for *Dinosaurs by Year,* in order of the date the dinosaur was first discovered (or a paper about it was first published), or in terms of *World Records,* like the biggest, smallest, fastest, dumbest, and so on. *Special Topics* include Ages of the Mesozoic (details the time periods during the so-called Age of Reptiles), Paleo-Maps (the dance of the continents), Anatomy (skeletal diagrams), Non-Dinosaurs (animals often thought of as dinosaurs), a *Glossary,* and *FAQ.* These files are cross-referenced with 515 images by twenty-eight artists (by last count), all of which can be viewed in the *Art Gallery.* (Click on the thumbnail to see the full image. Click on the name link to read more about the featured dinosaur.)

Keesey recently redesigned the Dinosauricon, which he admits is not as nice-looking as the original version but downloads much more quickly on many different kinds of browsers. He will someday design a better site for faster modems and connections. You can subscribe to his E-mail list for updates. Mike is a computer dino-artist himself, and you can see his 2-D and 3-D images in the *Art Gallery,* or by entering *The Keesey Gallery* by clicking on one of the asteroids on the index page.

CHAPTER 7

MAJOR MUSEUMS AND PARKS

Academy of Natural Science Museum
www.acnatsci.org/dinosaurs/

RATING

Want to see some really big dinosaurs? This is the place!

The academy's Dinosaur Hall tour starts you off with a really scary and informative look at *Giganotosaurus*, the largest land predator ever found. At forty-five feet in length, this big, toothy fellow was about the size of a city bus—and a lot more dangerous. Remains of this extraordinary creature were recently discovered in Argentina, and the jaws set in its six-foot-long skull were powerful enough to chew up and swallow anything it encountered. Better hope those steak knife–like teeth stay on the other side of your screen!

From *Giganotosaurus* it's on to *T. rex*—everybody's favorite dinosaur—then to the academy's famous Time Machine, Paleo-lab, and Mesozoic Mural, depicting the entire 160-million-year span (Triassic through Cretaceous) of prehistory dominated by the dinosaurs. You won't want to miss the museum's dinosaur gift shop, where you can order actual fossils on-line.

Not surprisingly, there is a lot more at this site than just dinosaurs—if that weren't enough. Go back to the home page for an overall look at Philadelphia's Academy of Natural Science, one of America's oldest and most prominent scientific institutions. During the nearly two centuries since it was founded in 1812, the academy has gathered under its roof more than twenty-five million specimens of all kinds. Happily for dino-hunters like us, the museum is especially rich in dinosaur materials. The fossils, mounted skeletons, and murals on display here can whisk you right back to the Mesozoic Era when dinosaurs walked the earth.

The next time you are in the city of Benjamin Franklin, you'll want to visit the academy and walk through its not-so-virtual Dinosaur Hall with its *Albertosaurus, Tyrannosaurus rex, Giganotosaurus,* and other monstrous carnosaurs. But of course, you don't have to actually be in Philadelphia to enjoy all these great dinosaur exhibits. Many of them can be found on the Web site, which includes color photographs of full-size dinosaur models and skeletons along with detailed descriptions of the displays. Highlights include an exciting on-line tour of Dinosaur Hall and a glimpse of the colossal Mesozoic mural by Philadelphia artist Bob Walters.

Among the other site features are fascinating pages devoted to the digs in the western United States, where many of the museum's fossils were discovered, and the paleolabs where these prehistoric remains were studied and prepared for display. There are also separate pages on dinosaur skulls and footprints as well as the shallow inland seas once roamed by great oceangoing reptiles such as *Plesiosaurus* and *Ichthyosaurus.*

Like many other dinosaur sites, this one includes a special *Kids' Section,* and teachers will find a section of their own with an on-line supplement to assist with lesson planning. Dino-surfers will want to check out the *Links* feature. It contains nearly fifty separate listings for Web sites ranging from Curse of the *T. rex* (see page 64), maintained by the PBS *Nova* science documentary series, to Zoom Dinosaurs (see page 45), an educational site for students of all ages.

ADDRESS AND PHONE NUMBER:
Academy of Natural Science Museum
1900 Benjamin Franklin Parkway
Philadelphia, PA 19103
(215) 299-1000

American Museum of Natural History
www.amnh.org/

You could spend weeks in the American Museum of Natural History without ever seeing anything twice. This museum of museums, located on Central Park West in New York City, really is *that* big. There are at least forty sizable halls and galleries, and sampling even a respectable fraction of them in any one visit is simply not possible. Six of the halls are devoted to prehistory and the Mesozoic Era, so dino-lovers can lose themselves for days in this place.

No wonder the American Museum is a mecca for dino-hunters. For starters, one of the most spectacular dinosaur exhibits in the world can be found in the Theodore Roosevelt Rotunda at the entrance. There a *Barosaurus* mother rears up to a height of nearly five stories to protect her young from a predatory *Allosaurus*. This 140-million-year-old drama has been so skillfully re-created, it is possible to forget that these are fleshless skeletons. Beyond the rotunda, the entire Mesozoic Era is played out before your eyes. You'll want to see all of this in person someday soon, but you'll need more than just a weekend visit to do anything but scratch the surface. Keep in mind that this museum offers many attractions in addition to dinosaurs.

Until your next trip to the Big Apple, you can satisfy at least some of your curiosity by plunging into the American Museum Web site—one of the most colorful and informative on the Internet. Accessible at the address listed above, it contains all the information you'll need to plan an enjoyable museum visit. But travel information is only a small part of what you'll find here. This Web site features handsomely illustrated displays on a wide variety of museum-related topics. Particularly attractive are its *Fifty Treasures* pages, offering a virtual tour of some of the museum's most important and best-known exhibits. Among these are color photographs and accompanying articles on the *Barosaurus*, dinosaur embryo, dinosaur mummy, dinosaur track, and *T. rex* displays. Also included—and not to be missed—are pages on the Star of India gem, Komodo dragon lizard, equine evolution, Cape York meteorite, Ice Age art, giant sequoia, blue whale, Tasmanian wolf, passenger pigeon, and mastodon.

ADDRESS AND PHONE NUMBER:
American Museum of Natural History
79th Street and Central Park West
New York, NY 10024
(212) 769-5100

Boston Museum of Science
www.mos.org

Visitors will find much to enjoy in this museum, since nearly every field of science receives some attention here. But for dino-hunters the highlight is likely to be the museum's recently acquired skull of *Giganotosaurus,* the humongous *T. rex*–type meat-eater discovered recently in Argentina's Northern Patagonia desert. The skull is six feet long and brandishes rows of daggerlike teeth capable of biting off half a ton of flesh at a time. The *Giganotosaurus* grew up to forty-five feet in length and weighed in at between eight and ten tons. The *Giganotosaurus* joins a one-and-a-half-story (anatomically obsolete) *Tyrannosaurus* model, a mounted *Triceratops* skeleton, *Apatosaurus* footprints from a trackway in Texas, and an array of other dinosaur fossils, casts, and models.

The museum Web page provides an on-line tour including a look at *Giganotosaurus* and some of the other dinosaurs found here. Both automatic and self-paced tours are available. While this site is not necessarily rich in dinosaurs, it will be of considerable interest to anyone fascinated by science.

ADDRESS AND PHONE NUMBER:
Boston Museum of Science
Science Park
Boston, MA 02114
(617) 723-2500

Buffalo Museum of Science

www.sciencebuff.org/
bms.buffnet/Dinosaurs/

Visitors could walk themselves to a frazzle in the ninety-three-thousand-square-foot Buffalo Museum of Science. Call up the Web sites above and maybe you can save some shoe leather.

The museum's life-size displays include *Allosaurus, Nanosaurus,* and *Triceratops,* as well as marine reptiles such as mosasaurs and early aviators such as the pterosaurs and *Archaeopteryx.* Unfortunately, you won't find much of this on the main museum site (www.sciencebuff.org)—which, incidentally, offers far too many options and not enough graphics.

ADDRESS AND PHONE NUMBER:
Buffalo Museum of Science
1020 Humbolt Parkway
Buffalo, NY 14211
(716) 896-5200

Calgary Prehistory Park

www.calgaryzoo.ab.ca/

Since dinosaurs have been extinct for sixty-five million years, you might not expect to find them at a zoo, but try out the Web site above, and you'll make a surprising discovery.

The Calgary Zoo in Alberta features an extensive Prehistoric Garden, complete with a herd of lifelike dinosaur models. On display in this amazing eighty-acre prehistoric wonderland are models of *Ankylosaurus, Apatosaurus, Corythosaurus, Edmontosaurus, Ornitholestes, Stegosaurus, Struthiomimus, Styracosaurus, Triceratops, Tyrannosaurus rex,* and many other dinosaurs, as well as 120-plus species of plants that give the illusion of a Mesozoic landscape.

The Calgary Zoo's Web site offers a colorful virtual tour of the garden with snapshots of its giants. There's also plenty of information on hand for anyone planning a trip to Calgary and its world-famous zoo. Make that trip if you can, since there may not be an experience anywhere quite like this one. A walk through the Prehistoric Garden will take you through 160 million years of earth history from the beginning of the Triassic Period, about 225 million years ago, down through the end of the Cretaceous Period.

The Calgary Zoo also offers a number of Zoofari Tours each year to exotic locations such as the East African plains or the Galápagos Islands. Because they provide excellent opportunities to study natural history and evolution, these may be of interest to dino-hunters.

ADDRESS AND PHONE NUMBER:

Calgary Zoo, Botanical Park and Prehistoric Garden
P.O. Box 3036, Station B
Calgary, Alberta, Canada T2M 4R8
(403) 232-9300
(800) 588-9993

California Academy of Sciences
www.calacademy.org/

RATING

On the California Academy of Sciences home page, you'll encounter the motto "Earth, Ocean, Space—All in one place!" Above the motto are logos for the Steinhart Aquarium, Morrison Planetarium, and Natural History Museum. The symbol for the latter is the head of a *T. rex*, so which logo are you likely to click on first? You guessed it—the big toothy one, but if you are looking for a herd of dinosaurs at this Web site, you are likely to be disappointed. The museum complex is so large that the official academy site can spare only limited space and time for any given subject—even for dinosaurs.

Even so, you should plan an academy visit the very next time you are in San Francisco. A world-class educational complex on a par with the Smithsonian in Washington, D.C., and the American

Museum of Natural History in New York, it attracts more than 1.5 million museumgoers each year. Indeed, you'll find your dinosaur herd right where it's supposed to be—in the Natural History Building. There are articulated skeletons of vicious meat-eaters such as *Allosaurus, Dilophosaurus,* and public enemy number one, *Tyrannosaurus rex.* The academy's "Life through Time," exhibition is a must, since it takes visitors on a 4.5-billion-year journey through the earth's turbulent history. Of course there is much more to see, so you'll want to budget your time accordingly. Take a virtual tour of the complex before you visit. The museum-map feature makes it easy. All you have to do is point and click on a room or subject of interest and you'll get a photograph and description of the offerings.

ADDRESS AND PHONE NUMBER:
California Academy of Sciences
Golden Gate Park
San Francisco, CA 94118
(415) 750-7145

Canadian Museum of Nature
www.nature.ca/

RATING

The Canadian Museum of Nature in Ottawa maintains both English and French versions of its Web pages. Regardless of which language you prefer, you'll find plenty of information and colorful illustrations in this site's delightful *Dinosaurs* (or *Les Dinosaures*) pages. These offer a glimpse of the "Life Through the Ages" exhibit to be found in the museum's Victoria Building. The exhibit contains numerous mounted skeletons, models, and fossil specimens of *Triceratops, Anchiceratops* (another horned plant-eater), *Styracosaurus, Daspletosaurus, Panaplosaurus* (a type of ankylosaur), and many other dinosaurs.

ADDRESS AND PHONE NUMBER:
Canadian Museum of Nature
P.O. Box 3443, Station D
Ottawa, Ontario, Canada K1P 6P4
(613) 996-3102

Carnegie Museum of Natural History
www.clpgh.org/cmnh/

Located in Pittsburgh, the Carnegie is one of our nation's finest museums, and naturally, dinosaurs are counted among its foremost attractions. The Carnegie's famed Dinosaur Hall whisks visitors away on an epic journey through the Triassic, Jurassic, and Cretaceous Periods, providing close encounters with giant sauropods such as *Diplodocus* and *Apatosaurus,* bird-hipped plant-eaters such as *Dryosaurus* and *Camptosaurus,* and fierce meat-eaters such as *Tyrannosaurus rex* and *Allosaurus.*

Like its public museums in Pittsburgh, the Carnegie's on-line exhibits are tops. While offerings change occasionally, there is usually at least one dinosaur exhibit featured on the Carnegie Web site. Other on-line exhibits touch on anthropology, archaeology, geology, and exploration. We highly recommend the site's *On-line Discovery Room* feature, which will challenge you to reassemble a scrambled pile of dinosaur bones, match fossil skeletons to their proper skulls, and pick out the impostors from a herd of real—and fake—dinosaurs.

ADDRESS AND PHONE NUMBER:
Carnegie Museum of Natural History
4400 Forbes Avenue
Pittsburgh, PA 15213
(412) 622-3131

Chicago Academy of Science
www.chias.org/

You won't see many dinosaurs at this Web site, but if you are interested in paleontology or any other field of science, you should pay it a visit. Dedicated to the "scientific literacy of all citizens," the Chicago Academy of Science is one of the oldest and finest educational institutions in the country, and everything done there is first rate. So, too, are the pages you'll see at the above address. Click on the *Paleontology* option to find out the academy's high-quality and extensive fossil holdings.

ADDRESS AND PHONE NUMBER:

Chicago Academy of Science
2060 North Clark Street
Chicago, IL 60614
(312) 871-2668

Cleveland Museum of Natural History
www.cmnh.org/

The Cleveland Museum of Natural History is a treasure trove of dinosaur materials. Among its paleontology exhibits are mounted specimens of *Allosaurus,* the duck-billed *Anatosaurus,* and a seventy-two-foot-long *Haplocanthosaurus.* There are also skulls or other fossils from *Stegosaurus, Triceratops,* the *T. rex*–like *Nanotyrannus,* and many other dinosaur species. Unfortunately, hardly any of these have made it onto the museum Web site, which, incidentally, is generally weak on graphics. However, the site contains one extraordinary feature that makes it a must for anyone researching dinosaurs on the Internet. Look under *Serious Fun!* for the *Dinosaur Internet mailing list.* There you will find years' worth of back-and-forth communications from scientists and paleontology buffs on a wide range of dinosaur-related topics.

ADDRESS AND PHONE NUMBER:

Cleveland Museum of Natural History
1 Wade Oval Drive
University Circle
Cleveland, OH 44106
(216) 231-4600

Dallas Museum of Natural History
www.dallasdino.org/

You can tell from the Web site address—dallasdino—that this site has the right stuff. Just click on *Dinoworld* and you are off on a fascinating tour of fossil holdings at the well-known Dallas Museum of Natural History. Founded in 1936, the museum boasts a collection of more than 280,000 fossils and other specimens. Among the many impressive displays is a *Tenontosaurus,* celebrated as the state's first mounted dinosaur skeleton. Also on exhibit here are *Mosasaurus* and *Glyptodon,* along with fossils of countless other amazing prehistoric creatures. There are dinosaur tracks, as well as prehistoric fish, trilobites, and plenty of Cenozoic mammals. Much of this can be sampled at the Web site.

ADDRESS AND PHONE NUMBER:
Dallas Museum of Natural History
3535 Grand Avenue
P.O. Box 26193
Dallas, TX 75226
(214) 421-3466

Denver Museum of Natural History
www.dmnh.org/

When you bring up the Denver Museum of Natural History home page, you'll be greeted by the motto "So Many Adventures in One Place." In fact, this terrific Rocky Mountain museum has much to offer, and its Web pages provide an intriguing sampling. Check them out.

Long known for its impressive fossil displays and meticulously crafted dioramas depicting both modern and prehistoric wildlife, the museum now houses one of the nation's finest natural history exhibits. Called "Prehistoric Journey," it is by far the museum's largest and most ambitious permanent exhibition. Covering some seventeen thousand square feet of floor space, it took more than six years and $7.7 million to create. It includes a working fossil laboratory with public viewing area. The exhibition retraces earth's 4.5-billion-year history and tells the story of the appearance and evolution of life on the planet. Naturally, dinosaurs play an important role in this rather all-encompassing story and are pretty much the stars of the show. Unfortunately, you'll catch only a glimpse of all this on the *Exhibits* pages.

Even so, there's plenty here to see and enjoy, such as an innovative videocam feature. Give it a try. And if you are interested in doing your own research, click on the *Certification in Paleontology* option. The museum operates a certification program for paleontology lab- and field work, with courses taught by museum curators and associates.

ADDRESS AND PHONE NUMBER:
Denver Museum of Natural History
2001 Colorado Boulevard
Denver, CO 80205
(800) 925-2250
(303) 370-6387
(303) 370-6303 (for courses)

Dinosaur National Monument
www.nps.gov/dino/

If you haven't come across this site during your Internet dinosaur searches, then you aren't really trying. Dinosaur National Monument is the heartland of dinosaur country and a magnet for all dino-lovers, both professional and amateur. If you are planning a visit, a stop at this National Park Service Web site is a must. And if you can't go anytime soon, the monument pages are still worth a look. They offer beautiful photography, maps, and options for lodging, hiking, and river trips. There are also hyperlinks to sites with in-depth information on early exploration of the area, the dinosaurs who once lived here, and the Morrison Rock Formation where most of their remains were found.

The monument story is an exciting one. In 1909, a paleontologist, explorer, and fossil prospector named Earl Douglass discovered an amazing cache of fossilized dinosaur bones in this area. They emerged from reddish (Morrison) rocks, which were deposited here by a river about 150 million years ago. Among the 350 tons of fossil remains that Douglass eventually dug out of these hills were the remains of *Allosaurus, Apatosaurus, Barosaurus, Camarasaurus, Camptosaurus, Ceratosaurus, Diplodocus, Dryosaurus, Stegosaurus, Torvosaurus,* and many other Jurassic creatures.

If you visit the monument nowadays—and if you're serious about dinosaurs, you really should—you'll see many of the fossils Douglass and others discovered here. The Dinosaur Quarry Visitors Center, about seven miles north of Jenson, Utah, features a dramatic exhibit of more than sixteen hundred dinosaur bones covering one entire wall of the center, as well as an on-site laboratory where quarried fossils are cleaned and prepared for exhibit, which is open to the public.

In all, this dino-hunter's paradise encompasses more than 210,000 acres and offers endless opportunities to learn and explore. There are many highly educational drives and hikes within the monument. One of the best ways to experience this extraordinary area and its prehistoric riches is by water along the tumbling Green and Yampa Rivers. Check with the Web site for the names and numbers of commercial white-water guides.

ADDRESS AND PHONE NUMBER:

Dinosaur National Monument
P.O. 210
Dinosaur, CO 81610
(303) 374-2216

Dinosaur National Monument
P.O. Box 128
Jensen, UT 84035
(801) 789-2115

Dinosaur Provincial Park

www.gov.ab.ca/env/parks/prov_parks/dinosaur/

You may spend a lot of time typing the address above—make sure you spell it out correctly—but you'll find the site well worth the effort. It is so large and so packed with information and photography that you can surf around inside it for an hour or more. You'll learn about how nature formed the Alberta badlands where Dinosaur Provincial Park is located and get a close-up introduction to many of the prehistoric species that once lived here. Complete and partial skeletons of *Albertosaurus, Centrosaurus, Corythosaurus, Elmisaurus* (a Late Cretaceous theropod), *Kritosaurus* (a Cretaceous duckbill), *Lambeosaurus, Ornithomimus, Stegoceras* (a small, Late Cretaceous plant-eater), *Styracosaurus* (a four-legged, bird-hipped plant-eater with head spikes), and many other dinosaur species have been recovered in the park. The fossil-bearing formations date from the Late Cretaceous about seventy-five million years ago, when the climate in this area was not very Canadian at all. Instead, it was much more like that of northern Florida today. Rivers flowed eastward toward a shallow sea, and their warm, swampy floodplains provided a perfect environment for dinosaurs.

ADDRESS AND PHONE NUMBER:
Dinosaur Provincial Park
P.O. Box 60
Patricia, Alberta, Canada T0J 2K0
(403) 378-4342

Field Museum of Natural History

www.fmnh.org/

Created in 1893 to serve as an attraction of the famed Colombian Exposition, Chicago's Field Museum is one of the nation's oldest and best scientific institutions. Dinosaurs have always been a big attraction at the Field, and today the museum continues to fascinate visitors with dinosaur fossils, casts, mounted skeletons, and models. *Albertosaurus, Apatosaurus* (once known as *Brontosaurus*), and *Brachiosaurus* are among the standouts in Dinosaur Hall, which was remodeled as part of the museum's centennial in 1994. Examples of these museum holdings can be sampled on the Field's excellent Web site.

The good folks at the Field are especially proud of a recent—and highly publicized—acquisition, a toothy *Tyrannosaurus rex* with the unlikely name of Sue. An entire section of the Web site is devoted to Sue, said to be the most complete dinosaur skeleton ever collected. Sue was uncovered near the little town of Faith, South Dakota, in 1990, and very soon became the object of a tug of war between several prospective owners and the U.S. government. Eventually purchased by the Field Museum, she is now on permanent display at the museum. Approximately 90 percent—an extraordinarily large portion—of Sue's fossilized bones were recovered, and this is allowing scientists to study the *T. rex* as never before. Only twenty-two other *T. rex* skeletons have been discovered, and none is as complete as Sue.

An especially delightful feature of the Field Web site is the *Sue Web Camera,* which provides a live shot of the museum's paleolab. Also of note is a revolving "Dinosaur of the Month" exhibit providing a close-up look at various dino types. Also, don't miss the museum store, where you can order on-line some excellent fossil reproductions at very reasonable prices.

ADDRESS AND PHONE NUMBER:
Field Museum of Natural History
Roosevelt Road at Lake Shore Drive
Chicago, IL 60605
(312) 922-9410

Fort Worth Museum of Science and History

www.fwmuseum.org/

This Fort Worth Museum Web site offers at least two top-quality on-line exhibits. One of these features a variety of Lonestar Dinosaurs, including *Tenontosaurus,* perhaps the state's best-known and -loved prehistoric creature. The other takes cybervisitors on a walk through the museum's innovative DinoDig exhibit.

The DinoDig allows museumgoers to conduct their own excavations in a replica of an actual Texas fossil quarry containing casts of real *Tenontosaurus* fossils. To make sure the DinoDig experience is true to life and scientifically accurate, museum staffers have consulted extensively with Dr. Louis Jacobs. There is an added touch of fantasy, however, since full-size dinosaur models keep watch over amateur paleontologists while they work. You can read all about it—and see it for yourself—at the Web site.

ADDRESS AND PHONE NUMBER:
Fort Worth Museum of Science and History
1501 Montgomery Street
Fort Worth, TX 76107
(817) 732-1631

Harvard Museum of Natural History

www.hmnh.harvard.edu
www.mcz.harvard.edu/

A separate section of the Harvard Museum is known as the Museum of Comparative Zoology, and it is there you'll find the dinosaurs. Visitors will encounter a forty-two-foot-long *Kronosaurus* (a rather vicious-looking marine reptile), as well as an almost endless array of Mesozoic fossils. The *Triceratops* skeleton seen here was among the first ever discovered. Also on display are mounted skeletons of *Deinonychus, Allosaurus, Plateosaurus* (an early sauropodlike plant-eater), and several other dinosaurs, as well as the flying reptile *Pteranodon* and the sail-backed *Dimetrodon.*

Unfortunately, you won't necessarily see all of these wondrous things on the museum's Web site. Dinosaurs are mentioned but not highlighted on the sites listed above. Perhaps the Museum of Comparative Zoology site (www.mcz.harvard.edu/), which remains under construction at this time, will offer more on-line dinosaur materials in the future. Meanwhile, check out the museum's on-line educational and travel offerings. One recent series of family programs was called *Digging for Dinosaurs* and gave parents a chance to explore the dinosaur phenomenon with their children.

ADDRESS AND PHONE NUMBER:
Harvard University Museums
26 Oxford Street
Cambridge, MA 02138
(617) 495-3045

Houston Natural Science Museum
www.hmns.mus.tx.us/

This Web site is almost as colorful and diverse as the museum complex it represents, which includes numerous educational attractions, such as a planetarium, observatory, and Imax theater, as well as several exhibit halls. The Houston Natural Science Museum is one of the nation's finest educational attractions. Unfortunately, there is so much here, the site devotes only a little space to each of its attractions. Alas, the same is true of the museum's dinosaur holdings.

The museum itself contains an extensive dinosaur display within its nine-thousand-square-foot "Life Through Time" exhibition. The Web site—essentially, an advertisement for the entire science complex—devotes only a couple of pages to the museum's Paleontology Hall. Even so, there's plenty here to convince casual

Internet surfers, as well as devoted dino-hunters, that they really must visit this museum.

The next time you visit Houston, put this fine science facility on your schedule, and be sure to set aside plenty of time for exploring "Life Through Time." A fifty-foot, backlit mural by William Stout provides an excellent starting point. Many of the creatures shown in the 4.5 billion years depicted in the mural turn up in fossil displays elsewhere in the hall. At the heart of the hall is its Mesozoic section, where you'll encounter a seventy-eight-foot-long *Diplodocus* skeleton and a twenty-eight-foot real-fossil mount of a duck-billed *Edmontosaurus* as well as a forty-five-foot-long model of *Tyrannosaurus rex.* A thrilling Cretaceous diorama shows a predatory *Dromaeosaurus* leaping from a cliff face in pursuit of an *Ankylosaurus.* The hall also features models, casts, and fossils of *Archaeopteryx, Deinonychus, Quetzalcoatlus, Stegosaurus,* and many other types.

ADDRESS AND PHONE NUMBER:
Houston Natural Science Museum
One Hermann Circle Drive
Houston, TX 77030
(713) 639-4600

Milwaukee Public Museum
www.mpm.edu/

Creative exhibits have always been a hallmark of the Milwaukee Museum. The original museum, built in 1882, contained one of the first total-habitat dioramas—showing a family of muskrats in their natural surroundings. Although quite familiar to museumgoers nowadays, this type of display was considered highly innovative at the time. It became known as the "Milwaukee style" and can still be seen in museum dioramas around the country.

No less innovative today, the Milwaukee Museum contains a wealth of high-tech, interactive displays that bring geography, history, science, anthropology, archaeology, geology, and paleontology to life for visitors. And with its dinosaur displays, the museum pushes its century-old environmental style well into the twenty-first century. In an exhibition known as "Third Planet," mounted skeletons and models of *Stegosaurus, Triceratops, Tyrannosaurus,* and many other dinos are shown in what are believed to have been their native habitats.

Naturally, the museum Web site is also exceptional and includes a virtual avalanche of material on dinosaurs, dinosaur extinction, and fossils. Once you've reached the museum Web site, the Third Planet feature is the place to go. Take the virtual tour, and you'll be treated to a walk through time beginning with the origin of the earth some 3.8 billion years ago, passing through the Age of the Dinosaurs, and moving right on up to the Ice Ages and the present. The museum's geology department has its own separate Web site. Both sites can be accessed at the Web address above.

ADDRESS AND PHONE NUMBER:
Milwaukee Public Museum
800 West Wells Street
Milwaukee, WI 53233
(414) 278-2702 (recorded information)
(414) 278-2700 (receptionist)

Natural History Museum of Los Angeles County
www.nhm.org

This natural history showplace is one of the finest museums in the world, and not surprisingly, it offers one of the best and most exciting exhibits on the Internet. The on-line dinosaur exhibit features *Albertosaurus, Apatosaurus, Euoplocephalus, Tenontosaurus,* and many other denizens of the Mesozoic Era. You can point and click to any one of these dinos and get a terrific full-color illustration and hot links to other sites offering more information. So, if you are doing on-line dinosaur research, the Natural History Museum of Los Angeles site is a good place to start.

The museum itself is well worth a visit. Its exhibits on sharks, birds, gems, and Native American cultures can keep you interested and entertained for days. The same can be said for its paleontology displays, which include many permanent dinosaur exhibits, such as a complete skeleton cast of the long-necked and dramatic full-size models of *Allosaurus* and *Carnotaurus* (an Early Cretaceous meat-eater). Especially impressive is an enormous *Tyrannosaurus rex* skull, one of the few on view in any public museum.

ADDRESS AND PHONE NUMBER:

Natural History Museum of Los Angeles
900 Exposition Boulevard
Los Angeles, CA 90007
(313) 744-3426

National Museum of Natural History
(Smithsonian Institution)
www.nmnh.si.edu/

Just as one might expect, the Smithsonian hosts an impressive Web page. The virtual tour of the natural history museum includes a very colorful and informative section on dinosaurs. A little surfing within the site will also get you to the Dinosaur Hall feature where you'll enjoy some great photographs of dinosaur fossils and dioramas including a fierce-looking *Allosaurus.*

The museum's on-line tour is not limited to dinosaurs, and you can spend hours skipping from one enjoyable display to the next. Of course, what you'll see here is the merest sampling of what the real Smithsonian in Washington, D.C., has to offer. Often described as "America's Attic," the Smithsonian Institution long ago earned its reputation as our nation's foremost museum complex. Stretching for nearly a mile along both sides of the Capitol Mall in Washington, D.C., are stone, brick, and marble Smithsonian museums celebrating history, air and space exploration, art, and science. It has been said that it would take an entire lifetime to do justice to every exhibit at the Smithsonian. However, dinosaur lovers will know, at least, where to begin. They know they are in the right place when they catch sight of Uncle Beazley, the bronze *Triceratops* just outside the National Museum of Natural History.

An entire hall on the main floor of the museum is devoted to dinosaur dioramas, skeletons, skulls, and other fossil materials. There are so many fossil mounts here that you may feel as if you are standing in the midst of a whole herd of dinosaurs. Among the highlights of the Dinosaur Hall are an eighty-seven-foot-long *Diplodocus longus,* a grimacing *Allosaurus,* threatening even as a skeleton, and a full-size *Stegosaurus* with bony back plates and spiked tail, not to mention *Albertosaurus, Brachyceratops, Camarasaurus, Camptosaurus, Ceratosaurus, Edmontosaurus, Maiasaura, Triceratops, Tyrannosaurus rex,* and countless other mounted skeletons, models, skulls, tracks, casts, and fossils.

Of course, the reach of this museum extends far beyond the Mesozoic Era. For instance, visitors will find an abundance of Cenozoic exhibits including rare early mammals and Ice Age giants such as the mammoth and mastodon—few museumgoers will forget the titanic elephant on display at the entrance. In fact, there are informative exhibits on every era of prehistory and practically every aspect of paleontology. The National Museum provides a solid grounding in the principles of paleontology as a science and in the development of dinosaurs as a species.

It would be a shame to visit the Smithsonian without taking the time to visit a few of its other halls, museums, and galleries. Even the most dedicated and single-minded dino-hunter is likely to feel the magnetic pull of their many attractions, so leave plenty of time to enjoy them. Of course, you won't be able to see everything.

ADDRESS AND PHONE NUMBER:
National Museum of Natural History
Tenth Street and Constitution
Washington, DC 20560
(202) 357-1300
(202) 357-2020 (for recorded travel information)

Peabody Museum of Natural History
www.peabody.yale.edu/

The colorful home page of this Web site makes it quite clear that you are entering dinosaur country. Worked into the Peabody Museum logo is the leaping skeleton of a *Velociraptor*. Remember those awful critters in that frightening *Jurassic Park* kitchen scene? Those were *Velociraptors*, or at least a moviemaker's conception of them. Below the logo is an illustration lifted from the Peabody's famous *Age of Reptiles* mural. Completed during the 1940s, the mural contains an artist's conception of the age of dinosaurs. Naturally, our vision of the distant past has changed during the half century between the painting of the mural and the making of the movie, and it's fun to compare these two imaginary dipictions.

Imagination—and dinosaurs—had a lot to do with the creation of the Peabody in the first place. The museum was established in 1866 with an endowment provided by banking tycoon George Peabody, the uncle and benefactor of O. C. Marsh, a man absolutely obsessed with dino-hunting. A Yale professor and noted paleontologist, Marsh stored his vast collection of fossils at the Peabody Museum. Many of the fossils he and his teams of devoted Yale students discovered more than a century ago can still be found there, and a few are pictured on the Web site.

Among the most imformative Peabody Web site features are its on-line exhibits. A long list of them can be accessed through the *Exhibits* option. An especially exciting and scientifically current one is the exhibit of "China's Feathered Dinosaurs." Featured here are fossils of *Confuciusornis* and several other Carboniferous dinosaurs. The fossil groups show the clear impressions of feathers and suggest that these early dinos were linked to modern birds.

Elsewhere you'll find plenty of information on the Peabody's permanent exhibits and collection. Don't leave the site without reading more about Marsh and the "Bone Wars" he fought with other paleontologists over fossil discoveries in the West. Incidentally, it was Marsh who identified many of the dinosaur types, such as *Apatosaurus, Stegosaurus,* and *Triceratops,* familiar to today's dino-hunters.

You should also plan to spend some time with the on-line mural exhibit. There you'll learn much about Rudolph Zallinger, the artist who painted the 110-foot-long mural depicting three hundred million years of earth history from Devonian times right down through the Cretaceous. An especially delightful feature allows you to click on various parts of the mural to get detailed information on particular aspects of prehistory. This certainly ranks among the most interesting scientific displays on the Internet.

ADDRESS AND PHONE NUMBER:
Peabody Museum
Yale University
170 Whitney Avenue
New Haven, CT 06520
(203) 432-5050

Petrified Forest National Park
www.nps.gov/pefo/

The Petrified Forest National Park Web site contains less information than some of the other National Park Service sites. It is handy for anyone planning a visit to the park, but not much help if you are looking for dinosaur stuff. After all, dinosaurs are not the center of attention here, but rather, the beautiful 250-million-year-old petrified wood. Even so, anyone fascinated by paleontology or natural history should be riveted by this almost mystical landscape and the extraordinary story it has to tell.

Approximately 225 million years old, the massive, petrified logs one sees here date to the Triassic Period, near the beginning of the Dinosaur Age. When they were living, these giant trees stood more than 250 feet tall and looked much like modern Norfolk Island pines. A major natural cataclysm such as a volcanic eruption or flood knocked the trees down and then covered them with silt. Eventually, the organic cells in the wood were filled with rocky minerals, forming the stony logs we see today.

Park visitors will see a lot more than just petrified logs, however. The park's Rainbow Forest Museum has on display many dinosaur fossils and dioramas depicting the area as it might have looked hundreds of millions of years ago when its trees were still growing and this part of Arizona was a vast swamp. The entire area was alive with lush vegetation and crawling with reptiles such as the crocodilelike phytosaur and *Staurikosaurus*, a meat-eating ancestor of the *T. rex*. The fossilized bones of a *Staurikosaurus*—an eight-foot-tall specimen nicknamed Gertie—are on display at the museum. Unfortunately, you won't see Gertie at the Web site.

ADDRESS AND PHONE NUMBER:

Superintendent
Petrified Forest National Park
P.O. Box 2217
Petrified Forest National Park, AZ 86028
(520) 524-6228

Royal Ontario Museum
www.rom.on.ca/

Like the Smithsonian Institution in Washington, D.C., the Royal Ontario Museum contains one of the world's greatest educational collections. More than six million specimens, artifacts, and other objects are housed there. Of course, the Royal Ontario's Web site is not as extensive as the museum itself, but it is, nonetheless, quite large. Navigating it is an adventure, and searching for information on the dinosaur collection is a bit like an expedition to the Canadian wilds. It's hard to know just where to look. We recommend the *Discovery* option. Of special note are the museum fossil pages.

> ADDRESS AND PHONE NUMBER:
> Royal Ontario Museum
> Main Building
> 100 Queen's Park
> Toronto, Ontario, Canada MSS 2C6
> (416) 586-5549

Royal Tyrrell Museum of Paleontology
www.tyrrellmuseum.com/

If you are serious about dinosaurs, then the Royal Tyrrell Museum of Paleontology is a place you really must see. Of course, it's located in the Canadian Province of Alberta, and that's not exactly right next door for most of us. So, until you can make a trip to the museum itself—and you should—try visiting the Tyrrell's extraordinary Web site.

The Tyrrell's virtual tour is likely the best you'll see anywhere on the Internet. Not just a grab-bag sampling, it starts you off at the museum entrance and takes you step-by-step through each major exhibit group. Once you're done—and your virtual journey can take up to an hour—you'll feel you know this museum. You'll also have a solid grounding in the fossil heritage of western Canada.

The museum has dozens of fine mounted skeletons such as *Centrosaurus, Coelophysis, Corythosaurus, Hadrosaurus, Lambeosaurus, Ornitholestes,* and *Tyrannosaurus,* and you'll see many of them during your virtual tour. A special highlight is a subadult *Albertosaurus* (a *Tyrannosaurus*-like meat-eater named for the province). Many of these specimens came from Dinosaur Provincial Park, also in Alberta, and other digs throughout western Canada.

To fully understand fossil exhibits like those above requires a solid foundation in the earth sciences. Both the museum and its Web site offer a wealth of information on subjects such as continental drift, the formation of sedimentary rock, the evolution of species, reef formation, and fossil conservation, as well as paleontology. All of this makes the Tyrrell Web site an excellent place to begin your dinosaur explorations of the Internet.

ADDRESS AND PHONE NUMBER:
Royal Tyrrell Museum of Paleontology
P.O. Box 7500
Drumheller, Alberta, Canada T0J 0Y0
(403) 823-7707

St. Louis Science Center/Dinosaur Park
www.slsc.org/

RATING

The St. Louis Science Center Web site is quite large. It offers an excellent on-line gallery and tour and more than three hundred separate pages of information illustrated by upward of 150 color photographs. However, it may take a bit of surfing inside the site to reach the museum's biggest attractions—its dinosaur exhibits—but the effort will pay off handsomely. With patience you will eventually locate colorful pages on *Triceratops,* dinosaur skin, the Cretaceous mass extinctions, and much more. You'll also get a look at the center's popular Dinosaur Park just outside the main building.

Of course, there is also plenty of information for anyone planning to visit the center, an expedition we can highly recommend. This place is a must-see for dino-lovers. Everyone who comes here wants to see the dramatic diorama featuring a *Tyrannosaurus* attacking a *Triceratops*, but there is much more. A substantial collection of dinosaur material can be found in the center's "Ecology and Environment Past and Present" exhibition, where there are many fossils and life-size robotic models on display.

If you go, pick a day when you can picnic outdoors in Dinosaur Park. The full-size models of *T. rex* and other dino-favorites provide a whole new perspective on a chicken sandwich. Those who would prefer to eat their lunch in the shadow of scientific giants rather than prehistoric ones can sit inside at the Einstein Cafe.

ADDRESS AND PHONE NUMBER:
St. Louis Science Center
5050 Oakland Avenue
St. Louis, MO 63110
(314) 289-4400

San Diego Museum of Natural History
www.sdnhm.org

The San Diego Museum of Natural History is one of the oldest and most vigorous educational institutions in the West. The museum has been gathering fossil specimens and artifacts for the better part of a century and can boast a large array of dinosaur materials. Pay the museum a cybervisit to find out more about its dinosaur exhibits and displays. You likely remember that San Diego was the city where an angry *Tyrannosaurus rex* went on a rampage in Michael Crichton's prehistory potboiler, *The Lost World*.

ADDRESS AND PHONE NUMBER:
San Diego Museum of Natural History
1788 El Prado
Balboa Park

P.O. Box 1390
San Diego, CA 92112
(619) 232-3821

Universal Studios Florida
www.uescape.com/

It should come as no surprise to anyone that the Universal Studios
Florida resort is all about the movies. Since Universal's most successful film ever was *Jurassic Park*—which ironically enough was
about a theme park—you will see plenty of mechanical dinosaurs at
this Web site. Click on the *Jurassic Park* link for videos.

ADDRESS AND PHONE NUMBER:
Universal Studios Florida
1000 Universal Studio Plaza
Orlando, FL 32819
(407) 824-4321

University of California Museum of Paleontology
www.ucmp.berkeley.edu/

You might consider making this the first stop on your personal Internet dinosaur expedition. The site is loaded with information and
valuable links to hot dinosaur Web pages. Surf around and there's
just no telling what you'll come across. There are award-winning
pages here on geology, evolution, phylogenetic systematics (don't
ask us what that means), and much more. Be sure to take a tour of
the *Virtual Museum of Paleontology.*

ADDRESS AND PHONE NUMBER:
University of California Museum of Paleontology

University of California
Berkeley, CA 94720
(510) 642-1821

Walt Disney World
www.disney.com

Neither the Disney Corporation nor its Web site are limited to just "Mickey Mouse stuff." Even so, you can bet you'll see plenty of Mickey and his friends when you visit the address listed above. Happily for dino-hunters like us, there are also more than a few dinosaurs—and not just the fantasy kind.

The Disney.com site is almost as action packed and sprawling as Disney World itself, so you may have trouble locating the dinosaur attractions. Not to worry. Just go up to the handy *Search* box, type in "dinosaurs" and click on *Go*. That'll get you a plethora of delightful hot-link selections, one of which is Dinoland USA, a part of Disney's Animal Kingdom attraction. At Dinoland, you can visit a fossil laboratory and the Disney Boneyard, a sizable collection of mounted fossils. At the Boneyard you can catch a live Web cam shot of the main display room. Other options provide a glimpse of additional Dinoland attractions, such as the Cretaceous Trail, Countdown to Extinction, and Dinosaur Jubilee, a celebration of early fossil discoveries. Also included is Tarzan Rocks, a blurb for a live stage show featuring Tarzan, Jane, and a troup of jungle gymnasts. In Dinoland? Oh well, this is Disney.

ADDRESS AND PHONE NUMBER:
Walt Disney World
P.O. Box 10040
Lake Buena Vista, FL 32830
(407) 824-4321

Wyoming Dinosaur Center
www.wyodino.org/

Most dinosaur Web sites and museums say very little about the hard fieldwork paleontologists must do to uncover fossils and expand our knowledge of the past. The Wyoming Dinosaur Center is quite different in this respect, as you'll discover when you visit the museum's Web site at the address above. There you'll find page after colorful page of information on active dinosaur quarries and the museum laboratories where local fossils are studied and prepared for display.

Want to do your own hands-in-the-dirt digging for dinosaur bones? The Dinosaur Center offers exciting opportunities for fossil-gathering expeditions. All are conducted under the guidance of paleontologists or expert fossil prospectors. Of course, to take part, you'll have to visit the center, which is located in Thermopolis, Wyoming. That may be a long way from your home computer screen, but if you love dinosaurs the trip will be well worthwhile.

The museum can boast over twelve thousand square feet of display space with perhaps a dozen major paleontology exhibitions. On display are fascinating full-size fossil mounts of *Allosaurus, Apatosaurus, Ceratosaurus, Triceratops, Tyrannosaurus rex, Utahraptor,* and dozens of other dinosaur types. The Web site includes all the information you'll need for planning your visit. Be sure to click on the *Dig for a Day* option. It will tell you all about the center's highly educational participatory fossil digs.

ADDRESS AND PHONE NUMBER:
Wyoming Dinosaur Center
P.O. Box 868
Thermopolis, WY 82443
(307) 864-DINO
(800) 455-DINO

CHAPTER 8

SMALLER MUSEUMS AND PARKS

Agate Fossil Beds National Monument
www.nps.gov/agfo

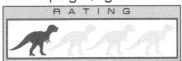

Once a huge cattle ranch, the three-thousand-acre Agate Fossil Beds National Monument is one of the world's richest sources of Miocene fossils. Some twenty million years ago, a mysterious disaster, likely a distant volcanic eruption, trapped thousands of animals by covering their bones with mud and sand. The fossilized bones are frequently under excavation, and visitors may very well see paleontologists hard at work here. From the visitor center, a two-mile trail leads to active fossil quarries. Get information for your visit from this typically excellent National Park Service Web site.

ADDRESS AND PHONE NUMBER:
Agate Fossil Beds National Monument
P.O. Box 27
301 River Road
Harrison, NE 69346
(308) 668-2211

Alabama Museum of Natural History
www.inusa.com/tour/al/tuscaloo/natural.htm

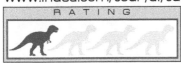

At the Alabama Museum of Natural History in Smith Hall, beside the historic campus quadrangle, visitors will find intriguing fossils dating from the Cretaceous Period down through the Ice Age. The Web site above provides some basic information on the museum and a glimpse of its main floor and rotunda.

ADDRESS AND PHONE NUMBER:

Alabama Museum of Natural History
P.O. Box 870340
Tuscaloosa, AL 35487
(205) 348-2040

Anniston Museum of Natural History
www.annistonmuseum.org

This colorful and well-constructed site offers an overview of the Anniston Museum of Natural History. Located at the gateway of the Southern Appalachians, believed by many to be the oldest mountains on earth, the museum celebrates our planet's 4.5-billion-year natural history. Dinosaurs and reptiles played a large role in the earth's history and, naturally enough, they are in evidence at the museum. Of particular interest to paleontology students and dino-buffs is a *Pteranodon* (a flying reptile) and a hungry-looking twenty-foot-long *Albertosaurus*. You'll get a sampling of the various galleries as well as travel information at the address above.

ADDRESS AND PHONE NUMBER:

Anniston Museum of Natural History
800 Museum Drive
Anniston, AL 36202
(256) 237-6766

Badlands National Park
www.badlands.national-park.com

As with many other National Park Web sites, this one gives you the feeling that you are going on a camping trip. As a matter of fact, if you decide to visit this out-of-the-way park, you'd best be prepared to camp, since Rapid City is a couple of hours away. Even so, every serious student of paleontology wants to visit this vast maze of barren buttes, pinnacles, and spires. Once a lush subtropical forest, and before that a shallow sea teeming with life, it is today one of the largest and richest fossil beds on earth. Most of the fossils here date to the late Cretaceous and Cenozoic Periods, and only a few of them contain the remains of dinosaurs.

ADDRESS AND PHONE NUMBER:
Badlands National Park
P.O. Box 6
Interior, SD 57750
(605) 433-5361

Big Bend National Park
www.big.bend.national-park.com/

Typical of National Park Service Web sites, this one provides a colorful and highly informative look at one of our country's foremost natural treasures. Big Bend National Park takes in more than eight hundred thousand acres of rugged Texas desert and mountains. Some southwestern Indians hold that when the Great Spirit had made the earth, all the leftover rocks were dumped into the Big Bend. Park visitors are likely to agree that sure enough, there are plenty of rocks here. This is a fact of considerable interest to dino-hunters, since some of the stone layers exposed here contain important fossils. For instance, the first fossils of the huge flying lizard *Quetzalcoatlus*

were found in the Big Bend by a University of Texas student. If all of this interests you, then so will the Web address listed above.

ADDRESS AND PHONE NUMBER:
Big Bend National Park
Big Bend National Park, TX 79834
(915) 477-2251

Big Bone Lick State Park
www.state.ky.us/agencies/parks/bigbone.htm

Big Bone Lick got its odd name because of the many huge bones pioneers found here. Early settlers often saw herds of bison and other large animals who came to lick the natural mineral deposits left by a prehistoric sulfur spring. Many of the bones they found were not those of modern animals but of mammoths, mastodons, and extinct sloths who had died here as many as twenty thousand years ago. Likely these hapless creatures were trapped by the sticky mud surrounding the spring. Their fossilized remains provide a glimpse of life toward the end of the last Ice Age. The park is made all the more delightful by life-size models of a mastodon and early bison. Sorry, no dinosaurs, but the huge, elephantlike mastodons are sure to impress.

ADDRESS AND PHONE NUMBER:
Big Bone Lick State Park
3380 Beaver Road
Union, KY 41091
(606) 384-3522

Black Hills Institute of Geological Research
www.bhigr.com/

Don't miss this one, dino-hunters! At this address, set up by scientists and professional fossil prospectors, you'll see the real thing—dinosaur bones only recently discovered, studied, and mounted.

A private, for-profit paleontological organization, the Black Hills Institute of Geological Research sells professionally prepared fossils and museum-quality cast replicas. The institute is a thriving concern, with sixteen geologists and fossil preparers on staff. Remarkably, institute experts have excavated five different *Tyrannosaurus rex* skeletons. Among these is "Stan," said to be the largest *Tyrannosaurus* skeleton ever mounted. You can download a very nice image of the menacing Stan, who looks as if he is about to spring into action.

ADDRESS AND PHONE NUMBER:
Black Hills Institute of Geological Research
P.O. Box 643
217 Main Street
Hill City, SD 57745
(605) 574-4289

Burke Museum of Natural History and Culture
www.washington.edu/burkemuseum/

Dino-hunters will find a lot to like at the Burke Museum of Natural History in Seattle. The "Dino Times" exhibit shows off a number of fine mounted skeletons, such as a *Stegosaurus,* an *Elasmosaurus,* and a 140-million-year-old *Allosaurus.* The neighboring "Cold Times" display focuses in on Ice Age materials, including a ten-thousand-year old mastodon skeleton, a saber-toothed cat, and a giant ground sloth.

You can get a good look at the displays by visiting the museum Web site.

ADDRESS AND PHONE NUMBER:
Burke Museum
Box 353010
University of Washington
Seattle, WA 98195
(206) 543-5590

Calvert Cliffs State Park
www.calvert-county.com/stateprk.htm

Here you'll find all the information you'll need for a visit to one of the most interesting fossil deposits in the East. At the Calvert Cliffs State Park, on Maryland's southern Chesapeake shoreline, is a thick layer of rich fossil material from the Miocene Epoch of about fifteen million years ago. Since these fossils were deposited long after the Mesozoic Era ended, there are no dinosaur remains here, but you can dig up some really fascinating stuff. Among the more popular finds are shark teeth. The often large and impressive teeth may survive more or less intact for millions of years after the rest of a shark's body has turned to clay. The cliffs are especially attractive to families with kids looking for souvenir reminders of primordial ocean marauders. Incidentally, you are allowed to keep any fossils you find here, but unfortunately, none are displayed at the Web site.

ADDRESS AND PHONE NUMBER:
Calvert Cliffs State Park
Merkle Wildlife Sanctuary
11704 Fenno Road
Upper Marlboro, MD 20772
(301)-8881410

Calvert Marine Museum
www.calvertmarinemuseum.com

This handsome and well-constructed Web site is almost as fascinating as the Calvert Marine Museum itself. One click on the *paleontology* bar will provide you with a wealth of information on fossils and prehistory in southern Maryland. The fossil page recounts the history of the shallow seas that covered this region for eons. Since this area was underwater throughout much of the Mesozoic Era, you won't find much in the way of dinosaur materials either at the Web site or the museum, but both can provide excellent background information on paleontology. Be sure to find out about the museum's fossil-gathering field trips.

ADDRESS AND PHONE NUMBER:
Calvert Marine Museum
P.O. Box 97
Solomons, MD 20688
(410) 326-2042

Children's Museum of Indianapolis
www.childrensmuseum.org

Wow! The kenetosaur is certainly a lot of fun. It's a dancing dinosaur puppet created by artist John Payne, and you can watch it swing and sway either at the Children's Museum of Indianapolis or at its Web site. Of course, there's a lot more than puppets at this address—try the *Coolections* feature.

If you are a kid over the age of three and under the age of ninety-three, and happen to be in Indianapolis, be sure to experience this museum. Outside, you'll be greeted by a full-size *Tyrannosaurus* model. Inside, you'll find a small but perfectly respectable collection of fossils, along with several articulated dinosaur skeletons and a mounted mastodon.

ADDRESS AND PHONE NUMBER:
> Children's Museum of Indianapolis
> 3000 North Meridian Street
> Indianapolis, IN 46208
> (317) 924-5431

Cincinnati Museum of Natural History
www.cincymuseum.org

You'll get plenty of information here on the wonderful museum complex located in Cincinnati's great old train station, but you won't see much in the way of dinosaur stuff. The paleontology collections in the city Museum of Natural History and Science emphasize the Ice Age, when bison, ground sloths, and saber-toothed cats roamed the Ohio Valley. But check the Vertebrate Paleontology Program, and you may find an opportunity to join a real dinosaur dig.

ADDRESS AND PHONE NUMBER:
> Cincinnati Museum of Natural History
> 1301 Western Avenue
> Cincinnati, OH 45203
> (513) 287-7000

Cranbrook Institute of Science
www.cranbrook.edu

About twenty-five miles from Detroit, the Cranbrook Institute offers exhibits and outreach programs in paleontology, astronomy, and other scientific fields. Find out about them at the site listed above. There is an especially ferocious *T. rex* skeleton on the exhibits page.

ADDRESS AND PHONE NUMBER:
Cranbrook Institute of Science
500 Lone Pine Road
P.O. Box 801
Bloomfield Hills, MI 48013
(313) 645-3200

Dakota Dinosaur Museum
www.dakotadino.com

You'll see a lot more dinosaur fossils and displays at this site than at many others operated by much larger and better-known museums. Click on the *Discovery* and *Educational Programs* options for some interesting art and information sheets on *Triceratops, Coelophysis,* and *Deinonychus.*

ADDRESS AND PHONE NUMBER:
Dakota Dinosaur Museum
200 Museum Drive
Dickinson, ND 58601
(701) 225-DINO

Daytona Museum of Art and Science
www.moas.org/

Florida was underwater during the Mesozoic Era, so you won't see dinosaurs here. However, you will learn a lot about marine fossils. Find out what this excellent Florida museum has to offer at the Web site above.

ADDRESS AND PHONE NUMBER:

Museum of Art and Science
1040 Museum Boulevard
Daytona Beach, FL 32114
(904) 255-0285

Dinosaur State Park
www.dinosaurstatepark.org

Although it may come as a surprise to many, Connecticut is definitely dinosaur country. Probably the finest dinosaur trackway in
the East can be found at Dinosaur State Park near the picturesque
town of Rocky Hill. The Web site contains bare-bones descriptions of the park and not much else. However, if you would like to
walk in a dinosaur's footsteps and are planning a visit to Connecticut, give it a look.

ADDRESS AND PHONE NUMBER:
Dinosaur State Park
West Street
Rocky Hill, CT 06067
(860) 529-8423

Dinosaur Valley State Park
www.tpwd.state.tx.us/park/dinosaur/dinosaur.htm

A very unfriendly looking *Tyrannosaurus* welcomes you to the
Dinosaur Valley State Park Web site. There is a lot to see and
read about here, so enjoy yourself. You get photographs, directions, advice on weather and lodging, and a complete rundown on
the local flora and fauna. There is also an on-line opportunity to
purchase a reproduction of a real dinosaur footprint.

Interestingly, this Glen Rose, Texas, state park is not rich
in fossils of the usual sort—the bones of long-dead creatures.

Instead, there is evidence here of a drama that took place perhaps 110 million years ago. Rock-hard footprints left in the streambed indicate that a sixty-foot-long sauropod passed this way. Apparently in pursuit was a twelve-foot-long meat-eating theropod. No one knows who won the race, but we can guess.

ADDRESS AND PHONE NUMBER:
Dinosaur Valley State Park
P.O. Box 396
Glen Rose, TX 76043
(254) 897-4588

Discovery Place

Billed as a "hands-on, minds-on museum," the 140,000-square-foot Discovery Place has become one of the South's major travel destinations, and it is easy to see why. Children love the Place, and they'll find the museum's Web site equally delightful. Go to the *Exhibits* page and you'll see why. There are separate options here waiting to whisk you away to a rain forest, an aquarium, an amateur radio center, a "Science in Motion" exhibit, and yes, a special dinosaur feature. The latter will introduce you to *Dimetrodon,* a pre-dinosaur reptile; *Stegosaurus,* with its bony plates; *Apatosaurus,* with its long, snaky neck; *Triceratops,* with its forty-inch horns; *Pachycephalosaurus,* with its thick skull; and everybody's favorite, the *Tyrannosaurus,* with its big bite. All of these big guys are represented at the museum by fierce-looking robotic models, and you'll catch a glimpse of them here.

ADDRESS AND PHONE NUMBER:
Discovery Place
301 North Tryon Street
Charlotte, NC 28202
(704) 372-6261

Falls of the Ohio State Park
www.cismall.com/fallsoftheohio/

The falls of the Ohio State Park, near New Albany, Indiana, contains one of the richest fossil deposits east of the Mississippi. For much of geological history, this part of the Midwest was covered by a shallow sea. The teeming life nurtured by the warm waters of this sea left behind fossil deposits hundreds, if not thousands, of feet thick. Some of these fossils date back four hundred million years to Devonian times, long before the appearance of the first dinosaurs. Today, you can visit the park and explore these extraordinary remains for yourself, but first, stop in at this Web site and read about them.

ADDRESS AND PHONE NUMBER:
Falls of the Ohio State Park
P.O. Box 1327
Jeffersonville, IN 47131
(812) 280-9970

Fernbank Museum of Natural History
Fernbank Science Center
www.fernbank.edu/

Anyone interested in science or dinosaurs owes these excellent Atlanta educational facilities more than a passing glance. At the Fernbank Museum of Natural History, they'll be treated to a twenty-foot-tall *Albertosaurus* dominating a room filled with dinosaur fossils. At the separate Science Center they'll enjoy a full-size model of an ostrichlike *Struthiomimus*, a *T. rex* skull, and much, much more, all housed in a nine-thousand-square-foot exhibit hall. The Fernbank Web pages provide a sampling of exhibits and programs, but not much of interest to dino-hunters. The Science

Center home page contains a rather dark image of a *Struthiomimus* model and display hall.

ADDRESS AND PHONE NUMBER:
Fernbank Museum of Natural History
767 Clifton Road NE
Atlanta, GA 30307
(404) 378-0127

Fernbank Science Center
156 Heaton Park Drive
Atlanta, GA 30307
(404) 378-4311

Florida Museum of Natural History
www.flmnh.ufl.edu/

This museum and its Web site have the right stuff. With the opening of its exciting new exhibition center in Powell Hall, the Florida Museum of Natural History, located on the University of Florida campus in Gainesville, has pushed the museumgoing experience into the twenty-first century and beyond. The Web site, like the museum itself, places emphasis where it belongs—on the *investigation* of the world of science.

The *Fossil Horse Cybermuseum* you'll find at this site is one of the best paleontology features on the Internet. With crisply written text and stunning graphics, it takes you through millions of years of equine evolution. Along the way you'll learn plenty about fossil hunting and the basic principles of paleontology. Also, don't miss the interactive *Gallery of Fossil Vertebrates*.

ADDRESS AND PHONE NUMBER:
Florida Museum of Natural History
P.O. Box 112710
University of Florida
Gainesville, FL 32611
(352) 846-2000

Florissant Fossil Beds National Monument
www.nps.gov/flfo/

The prehistoric materials at the Florissant Fossil Beds National Monument in Colorado date from about thirty-five million years ago, so there are no dinosaur remains here. Even so, this beautiful and incredibly rich fossil quarry is deeply fascinating to anyone interested in the past. Covered by ash from successive volcanic explosions, the fossils here paint an intriguing picture of Cenozoic life. The Web site offers an abundance of useful information for anyone planning a visit, but there are very few pictures.

ADDRESS AND PHONE NUMBER:
Florissant Fossil Beds National Monument
P.O. Box 185
Florissant, CO 80816
(719) 748-3253

Fossil Butte National Monument
www.nps.gov/fobu

The Fossil Butte National Monument is well named, since this part of Wyoming is particularly rich in prehistoric remains. Those found within the monument date mainly to the Early Cenozoic Period, about fifty million years ago, when a huge freshwater lake innundated the area. Since the dinosaurs were all gone by that time, their fossils are not found here. Nonetheless, paleontology buffs and rock hounds will find this place fascinating. The visitors center has a thirteen-foot Fossil Lake crocodile on display, as well as early bat remains and an extraordinary mass of fish fossils. The Web site provides plenty of travel information but only a brief description of the monument and its fossils.

ADDRESS AND PHONE NUMBER:
Fossil Butte National Monument
P.O. Box 592
Kemmerer, WY 83101
(307) 877-4455

Garden Park Paleontology Society Dinosaur Depot
www.coloradodirectory.com/dinosaurdepot/

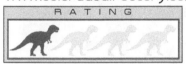

RATING

There may be no more-historic dinosaur quarry than the one near Canon City, Colorado, where a local naturalist came across a cache of mysterious bones in 1876. This discovery helped spark the famous Bone Wars of the late nineteenth century. The address above will be very useful to anyone planning to visit the area, but there are few, if any, pictures or descriptions of dinosaurs.

ADDRESS AND PHONE NUMBER:
Garden Park Paleontology Society/Dinosaur Depot
330 Royal Gorge Boulevard
Canon City, CO 81212
(719) 269-7150

Georgia Southern University Museum
www2.gasou.edu/musenews/

RATING

Maybe you think that big mouth in the movie *Jaws* was scary. Then try out the permanent exhibits page at the Georgia Southern University Museum Web site. In the background is the yawning jaw of a *Mosasaurus,* a fierce predator common to the primordial seas that once covered most of what is now known as the Peach State. The museum can boast a small but excellent collection of fossils, including the lower jaw of a *Tyrannosaurus rex* and a mounted *Mosasaurus* skeleton approximately twenty-six feet long.

Incidentally, opposing football teams may think there are prehistoric monsters on the Georgia Southern offensive line. The Eagles are a perennial favorite to win the NCAA Division I-AA national championship.

ADDRESS AND PHONE NUMBER:
Georgia Southern University Museum
U.S. 301
Statesboro, GA 30485
(912) 681-5444

Greensboro Natural Science Center
www.greensboro.com/sciencecenter/

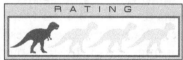

The Greensboro Natural Science Center boasts its own Dinosaur Gallery, complete with a thirty-six-foot model of *Tyrannosaurus rex*. You may or may not see the big *T. rex* on the museum Web site, but you'll find lots of helpful information for planning a visit in person. Be sure to check out the page dedicated to the museum store. It's called the Thesaurus Shop—a nice pun—and we're told you can purchase dinosaur models and real fossils there.

ADDRESS AND PHONE NUMBER:
Natural Science Center
4301 Lawndale Drive
Greensboro, NC 27455
(336) 288-3769

Hot Springs Mammoth Site
www.mammothsite.com

You'll find no better place on the Internet to learn about mammoths, those big, woolly prehistoric elephants. The art and information at this Web address are strictly first-rate. Readers should keep in mind, however, that mammoths were modern mammals and resembled dinosaurs in only one way—they were huge. As the park Web site explains, this is "where the big boys are," and that is true enough. More than fifty woolly and Colombian mammoths have been excavated from this one location—near Hot Springs, South Dakota. When they were alive some of them stood up to fourteen feet tall and weighed as much as eight tons.

ADDRESS AND PHONE NUMBER:
Hot Springs Mammoth Site
P.O. Box 692
Hot Springs, SD 57747
(605) 745-6017

Idaho State Museum of Natural History
www.isu.edu/departments/museum/

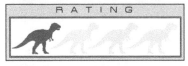

This is more or less a standard university museum site. Most of the fossils collected in the state of Idaho date to the Pliocene Period, long after dinosaurs had disappeared. So the locally gathered paleontology collections at the Idaho State Museum of Natural History in Pocatello are rather light on dinosaur remains. Even so, you may want to read here about the "Nature of Idaho" exhibit, where six hundred million years of local history are recounted. The giant bison skeleton is also worth a look.

ADDRESS AND PHONE NUMBER:
Idaho State University
Pocatello, ID 83209
(208) 236-3317

Illinois State Museum
www.museum.state.il.us/exhibits/

Drop in at this address for a glimpse of Illinois during the Ice Age (keep in mind that the dinosaurs were long gone by then). You can also view dozens of beautiful marine fossils. What you learn from this excellent on-line exhibit will be useful background for your dinosaur research.

ADDRESS AND PHONE NUMBER:
Illinois State Museum
Spring and Edward Streets
Springfield, IL 62706
(217) 782-7386

Jacksonville Museum of Science and History
www.jacksonvillemuseum.com/

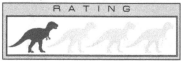

While the natural history holdings of this museum concentrate on local and marine fossils, there is an exciting *Allosaurus* skeleton on hand to greet and frighten visitors. Meat-eating dinosaurs of this type grew to thirty feet or more in length and are thought to have hunted in ferocious packs. Look for information on the *Allosaurus* skeleton and other museum holdings at the Web site. A particularly worthwhile museum feature is its "Ribbon of Life" exhibit, which explores the history and ecology of the Saint John River.

ADDRESS AND PHONE NUMBER:
Jacksonville Museum of Science and History
1025 Museum Circle
Jacksonville, FL 32207
(904) 396-MOSH

John Day Fossil Beds National Monument
www.nps.gov/joda/

The fossil record at the fourteen-thousand-acre John Day Fossil
Beds National Monument covers a period of approximately forty-
five million years, spanning much of the Cenozoic Era. Since the
dinosaurs were gone by the time the Cenozoic began, you won't
find their bones among these fossils. However, anyone with an
interest in paleontology—and that likely includes you—will love
this place. To plan your visit, stop in at this rather typical, though
high-quality, National Park Service Web site.

ADDRESS AND PHONE NUMBER:
John Day Fossil Beds National Monument
HCR 82, Box 126
Kimberly, OR 97848
(541) 987-2336

Johnston Geology Museum
www.emporia.edu/earthsci/museum/museum.htm

Although relatively small and not widely known, the Johnston
Geology Museum in Emporia, Kansas, is a first-rate facility. Maintained by Emporia State University, it is named for Dr. Paul Johnston, who taught earth sciences to students here for more than
thirty-eight years. Visitors will find an abundance of fossils and
other specimens, including a seventeen-foot Cretaceous mosasaur,

an eight-foot mastodon tusk, and a giant ground sloth. You can
see all these things and more by taking the museum's virtual tour,
which, in our opinion, is one of the best-designed on the Internet.

ADDRESS AND PHONE NUMBER:
Johnston Geology Museum
Emporia State University
200 Commercial Street
Emporia, KS 66801
(316) 341-5330

La Brea Tar Pits
George C. Page Museum
www.tarpits.org

The famed La Brea Tar Pits in Los Angeles yielded no dinosaurs,
but rather Ice Age creatures such as mammoths, saber-toothed cats,
and giant sloths that lived in this part of California between ten thousand and forty thousand years ago. The bones of thousands of such
creatures have been lifted from the sticky tar of the La Brea pits, and
of course, these are what you'll see when you visit the Web site.

ADDRESS AND PHONE NUMBER:
George C. Page Museum
5801 Wilshire Boulevard
Los Angeles, CA 90036
(323) 934-7243

Lexington Children's Museum
www.lexinfo.com/museum/children.html

The Lexington Children's Museum is a great place for kids interested in science in general and prehistory in particular. Young

visitors will find many fascinating fossil exhibits and plenty of dinosaur stuff. They can even do their own fossil prospecting. But don't expect too much from the Web site, as it provides little more than museum hours, directions, and telephone contacts.

ADDRESS AND PHONE NUMBER:
Lexington Children's Museum
401 West Main Street
Lexington, KY 40505
(606) 258-3253

Frank McClung Museum of Natural History
mcclungmuseum.utk.edu

This excellent Web site offers an overview of the McClung Museum of Natural History, part of the University of Tennessee at Knoxville. As you'll see, the McClung is a general-interest museum with no particular emphasis on natural history. Nonetheless, it offers some first-rate fossil displays. Go to the *Geology and Fossils* page for a sampling. You'll find a special section on the *Hadrosaurus,* which is not surprising since this duck-billed plant-eater is the only fossilized dinosaur ever found in Tennessee. However, the state has plenty of Ice Age fossils of creatures such as mastodons, giant sloths, dire wolves, giant beavers, and saber-toothed cats, and these are well represented at the McClung and on its Web site.

ADDRESS AND PHONE NUMBER:
Frank McClung Museum of Natural History
1327 Circle Park Drive
University of Tennessee
Knoxville, TN 37996
(865) 974-2144

McKinley Museum and National Memorial
www.mckinleymuseum.org

The McKinley Museum and National Memorial says it's "a hands-on museum, just don't feed the dinosaurs." That's a motto sure to attract kids and dino-hunters, and they won't be disappointed, since the McKinley Museum is home to "Alice," a robotic *Allosaurus*. Read about Alice and plan your visit at this Web site.

ADDRESS AND PHONE NUMBER:
McKinley Museum and National Memorial
800 McKinley Monument Drive NW
Canton, OH 44708
(330) 455-7043

McWane Center
www.mcwane.org

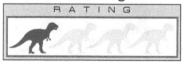

The McWane Center in Birmingham, Alabama, got its start as a pair of science facilities known as Discovery 2000 and the Red Mountain Museum. These merged in 1999 when the McWane Center on Nineteeneth Street was completed. The center offers an amazing array of interactive exhibits. The center's Web site has lovely graphics but is a bit hard to navigate. Give it a try anyway, and you'll learn about this exciting new science museum as well as Birmingham's Red Mountain. A ruddy seam of iron ore that runs through the mountain provided much of the raw material that made this southern city famous as a steel producer. The mountain is loaded, not just with iron ore, but with fossils providing clues to hundreds of millions of years of earth history. Many marine fossils have been found here, including the remains of giant, oceangoing reptiles.

ADDRESS AND PHONE NUMBER:
McWane Center
200 19th Street North
Birmingham, AL 35203
(205) 714-8400

Memphis Pink Palace Museum
Coon Creek Science Center
www.memphismuseums.org

You'll see plenty of fossils and dinosaurs at the Pink Palace Museum in Memphis. Unfortunately, you won't see them at this Web site. Still, that's no reason to skip the colorful and informative pages at this address. They'll tell you all about the museum's intriguing history and wide-ranging offerings. Of special interest is the Coon Creek Science Center, an associated educational center in McNair County, Tennessee. Here students are introduced to the art and science of fossil collecting.

ADDRESS AND PHONE NUMBER:
Memphis Pink Palace Museum
3050 Central Avenue
Memphis, TN 38111
(901) 320-6320

Mesa Southwest Museum
www.ci.mesa.az.us/

In addition to its extensive archaeological holdings, the museum houses a number of paleontology exhibits, including the popular "Jurassic Arizona." Read about it at the address above. You can also get information on the Southwest Paleontology Society, a volunteer organization associated with the museum. The society consists of amateurs and professionals interested in the field of paleontology, and of course, dinosaurs are an important focus.

ADDRESS AND PHONE NUMBER:
Mesa Museum Southwest
53 North MacDonald Street
Mesa, AZ 85201
(602) 644-2230

Michigan State University Museum
www.museum.msu.edu/

The Michigan State University Museum is so wide ranging that this Web site can devote only limited space to the subject of paleontology. Even so, you should check out the "Hall of Evolution," which can be reached via the *Exhibitions* option. Alas, what you won't find there are the museum's huge skeletons of *Allosaurus* and *Stegosaurus*. To see them, visit the museum itself next time you are in East Lansing.

ADDRESS AND PHONE NUMBER:
Michigan State University Museum
West Circle Drive
East Lansing, MI 48824
(517) 355-2370

Montshire Museum of Science
www.montshire.net

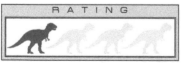

A hands-on facility, this museum in Norwich, Vermont, is a wonderful place for kids. It offers dozens of well-conceived exhibits on ecology, technology, natural history, and science. There's not much Mesozoic or Dinosaur Age material here, but you will find some excellent displays on more recent prehistory. The museum's Web site describes its Ice Age exhibit.

ADDRESS AND PHONE NUMBER:
Montshire Museum of Science
P.O. Box 770
Montshire Road
Norwich, VT 05055
(802) 649-2200

Morris Museum
www.morrismuseum.com/

Recently updated, this site provides a virtual tour of New Jersey's Morris Museum, where the most popular exhibition is, naturally enough, the Dinosaur and Fossil Gallery. Inside this spacious hall visitors will find five-hundred-million-year-old trilobites from the Cambrian Period. Not surprisingly, the gallery's most dramatic displays are from the Jurassic Period, which is well represented with a beautifully preserved *Ornitholestes* skeleton, *Stegosaurus* model, *Pteranodon* replica, and *Tyrannosaurus* skull.

ADDRESS AND PHONE NUMBER:
Morris Museum
6 Normandy Heights Road
Morristown, NJ 07960
(973) 538-0454

Morrison Natural History Museum
town.morrison.co.us/mnhm

The famed Morrison Rock Formation, which contains so many Late Jurassic fossils, takes its name from Morrison, Colorado, a small town just west of Denver. A massive outcropping of the reddish Morrison Formation can be seen just outside of town, and it was here in 1877 that schoolteacher Arthur Lakes found the fossils that touched off the great American Bone Wars. The address above will take you to the Morrison Natural History Museum, where displays recount the story of Lakes, his electrifying fossil discovery, and his relationship with bone warriors O. C. Marsh and E. D. Cope.

ADDRESS AND PHONE NUMBER:
Morrison Natural History Museum
P.O. Box 564
Morrison, CO 80465
(303) 697-1873

Museum of Northern Arizona
www.musnaz.org

The Museum of Northern Arizona displays cultural artifacts and natural history specimens from the Colorado Plateau, also known as the Four Corners, a region encompassing 130,000 square miles of mesas, canyons, and rocky, monumentlike buttes, often reddish in color. Countless valuable fossils have been found here, and you can see a nice selection of them at this museum. The Web site provides only a glimpse, however, so don't expect many dinosaur bones when you visit the address above. However, click on the *Exhibits* option and you will see a rather interesting mounted *Dilophosaurus.*

ADDRESS AND PHONE NUMBER:
Museum of Northern Arizona
Fort Valley Road
P.O. Box 720
Flagstaff, AZ 86001
(520) 774-5213

Museum of the Rockies
www.montana.edu/wwwmor/

No question about it, you'll want to take a virtual tour of the ninety-four-thousand-square-foot Museum of the Rockies in Bozeman, Montana. Of course, the highlights of the tour for dino-lovers will be the Earth Hall, Dinosaur Hall, and Fossil Bank. The theme of the entire museum complex is "One Place Through All of Time," so the exhibits concentrate on Montana fossil discoveries. There have been many of those, among the more significant being that of the *Maiasaura peeblesorum* (Good Mother Lizard), a dinosaur that apparently nurtured and cared for her young. Read about the *Maiasaura* here. Incidentally, the museum on-line store offers some great books and casts of fossil specimens.

ADDRESS AND PHONE NUMBER:
Museum of the Rockies
Montana State University
600 West Kagy Boulevard
Bozeman, MT 59717
(406) 994-2251 or (406) 994-3466

Naples Conservancy Nature Center
www.naplesdowntown.com/attrnatc.htm

This small but well-organized page offers a glimpse at some of the center's holdings, including its handsome natural history dioramas. Some of these contain fossils, but the real reason for visiting either the Web site or the museum itself is to get a better sense of the lush Florida natural environment. To those of us with active imaginations, the Florida landscape suggests Mesozoic times, when enormous sauropods tromped though marshes perhaps not unlike these.

ADDRESS AND PHONE NUMBER:
Naples Conservancy Nature
1450 Merrihue Drive
Naples, FL 33942
(813) 262-0304

Nebraska State Museum of Natural History
www-museum.unl.edu

This Web site would be worth a visit if only to see Mark Marcuson's extraordinary murals depicting the prehistory of the Midwest. You won't see any better dinosaur art on the Internet. However, there is much more here to interest the paleontology buff. In fact, you should set aside an hour or even a whole afternoon to take a virtual tour of the Nebraska State Museum of Natural History. Located on the University of Nebraska campus in Lincoln, this outstanding facility contains one of America's finest paleontology collections, and you will get a fascinating sample of it on the Web.

Known for its world-famous exhibition of mammoths, mastodons, and other prehistoric elephants, the museum features countless displays, many of them recalling the Age of Dinosaurs. Mounted skeletons include those of a *Stegosaurus* and *Allosaurus,* as well as large marine reptiles such as plesiosaurs and mosasaurs. Also on exhibit are skulls or partial skeletons of *Triceratops, Tyrannosaurus rex,* and many other dinosaurs, along with an abundance of material from the Cenozoic Era and the Ice Age.

ADDRESS AND PHONE NUMBER:
Nebraska State Museum of Natural History
Morrill Hall
University of Nebraska
Lincoln, NE 68588
(402) 472-2642

New Jersey State Museum

www.nj.com/dino/museum.html

For at least an hour's worth of dinosaur fun, look under "Old Bones" and click on *Dinos*, *Jersey Dino*, *Dino Day*, and *Dino Coupons*. The *Jersey Dino* bar tells the story of the duck-billed *Hadrosaurus* found near Haddonfield, New Jersey, in 1858. This was the first known dinosaur discovery made in the United States. A separate *Older Than Dinos* bar opens a page on "Older and Uglier" vertebrates, such as the tigerlike *Inostrancevia alexandri*, which predate the dinosaurs.

Don't stop with the bones! The museum and its Web site offer lots more than dinosaurs. Located in Trenton, the facility includes a planetarium, an auditorium, and a four-level exhibit building. Plan to visit if you can. The site provides plenty of information to help you make your travel plans.

ADDRESS AND PHONE NUMBER:
New Jersey State Museum
P.O. Box 530
205 West State Street
Trenton, NJ 08625
(609) 292-6464

New Mexico Museum of Natural History

www.nmmnh-abq.mus.nm.us/nmmnh/

Obviously, dinosaurs loved New Mexico, since they lived here for at least 160 million years. Dinosaur fossils were first collected in New Mexico during the 1880s, and they continue to be found today. The New Mexico Museum of Natural History in Albuquerque takes full advantage of the state's rich dinosaur heritage, and its dinosaur exhibits are among the finest in the Southwest.

You can take a virtual tour of the museum at the Web address above, but the chief attraction of this first-rate Web site is its *Dinosaurs in New Mexico* feature. It offers nearly two dozen options that provide a thorough introduction to the subject of dinosaurs in New Mexico. Read everything on the menu, and you'll come away with a true appreciation of the state's extraordinary dinosaur heritage. You'll find nicely illustrated articles on dinosaur eggs, skin, trackways, and much more. Included are paintings, maps, fossils, and glossaries. There is even a comprehensive dinosaur dictionary to help you spell some of those tongue-twisting names. For instance, try *Rioarribasaurus* (a Late Triassic theropod).

ADDRESS AND PHONE NUMBER:
New Mexico Museum of Natural History
1801 Mountain Road NW
Albuquerque, NM 87104
(505) 841-2800

New York State Museum
www.nysm.nysed.gov

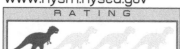

The New York State Museum in Albany was among the first public institutions to pursue research in paleontology. So it is ironic that neither the museum nor its Web pages are heavy with dinosaur materials. The museum contains a few fossil trackways and articulated skeletons.

ADDRESS AND PHONE NUMBER:
New York State Museum
State Education Center
Albany, NY 12230
(518) 474-5843

North Carolina Museum of Natural Science

www.naturalsciences.org

If you happen to be in Raleigh, North Carolina's capital city, don't pass up the chance to see this extraordinary museum. Among the newest—and at two hundred thousand square feet, among the largest—natural history facilities in the country, it can boast up-to-date exhibits and cutting-edge science. The Web site provides all the information you'll need for your visit.

When you go, take the museum tour and visit the breathtaking "Mountains to the Sea" exhibition. It takes you from the summit of the high Appalachians, through the Piedmont, and across the coastal plain to the Atlantic. Fossils and dioramas provide a glimpse at the state's prehistory, and you'll see replicas of *Tyrannosaurus rex, Triceratops,* and other prehistoric vertebrates. You'll get a colorful sampling of all this at the Web site.

ADDRESS AND PHONE NUMBER:
North Carolina Museum of Natural Science
11 W. Jones Street
Raleigh, NC 27601
(877) 462-8724

Oklahoma Museum of Natural History

www.omnh.ou.edu/

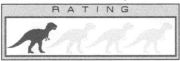

The new Sam Nobles Oklahoma Museum of Natural History is not yet complete and neither is its Web site. Nonetheless, be sure to check this address to see how work is progressing. No doubt, both the museum and the site will be extraordinary when they are finished. Dino-hunters will be especially interested, since many of the fine fossil discoveries made over the years in Oklahoma will likely find their way to the museum. No few of these were made by noted paleontologist J. W. Stovall, who was curator of the original museum.

ADDRESS AND PHONE NUMBER:
Oklahoma Museum of Natural History
2401 Chautaugua Avenue
Norman, OK 73072
(405) 325-4712

Orton Geological Museum
www.geology.ohio-state.edu/facilities/museum

Here you can download some excellent photographs of specimens on display at the Orton Geological Museum on the campus of Ohio State University in Columbus. One of these is the mounted skeleton of *Megalonyx jeffersoni,* a rather menacing giant sloth. Of course, this is not a dinosaur, but it is impressive enough to be one. You'll also see a full-size skull cast of a *Tyrannosaurus rex* as well as the head of a rather scary, twenty-foot-long Devonian fish. The big fish lived more than 360 million years ago, luckily for anglers, since no one would want to hook one like this.

The Web site provides a good overview of the museum for those who would like to visit. If you are traveling in Ohio, put this fine museum on your itinerary.

ADDRESS AND PHONE NUMBER:
Orton Geological Museum
Ohio State University
155 South Oval
Columbus, Ohio 43210
(614) 292-6896

Princeton Natural History Museum
www.princeton.edu/

The official Princeton Web site contains very little information about the university's natural history museum or the dinosaur skeletons on display there. Princeton, however, is a great place to visit and, of course, to get an education. Visit the site and have a look for yourself. If you do get a chance to visit the Princeton campus, don't miss the museum with its impressive *Tyrannosaurus, Allosaurus,* and *Maiasaura* remains. Mammal exhibits include fossils of the magnificent Irish elk, which became extinct in relatively recent times.

ADDRESS AND PHONE NUMBER:
Princeton Natural History Museum
Guyot Halls
Washington Street
Princeton University
Princeton, NJ 08544
(609) 258-1322

Redpath Museum
www.mcgill.ca/redpath/

Since it is open to the public on only a limited basis, this site may be your best opportunity for a glimpse of the famed Redpath Museum in Montreal. Established in 1882, the Redpath is used primarily as a research and teaching resource for McGill University. A relatively small facility, it was established to preserve and display the collections of a single man, noted naturalist Sir William Dawson. However, over the years it has grown to encompass nearly every aspect of paleontology, mineralogy, ornithology, mammology, invertebrate zoology, ethnology, and archaeology. A special feature here is the skeleton of a *Teleosaurus* (a Jurassic crocodile).

ADDRESS AND PHONE NUMBER:
Redpath Museum
McGill University
859 Sherbrooke West
Montreal, Quebec, Canada H3A 2K6
(514) 398-4086

Rennie Geology Museum
www.dickinson.edu/

Dinosaurs are scarce at this Dickinson College geology museum, but there is a rather amazing collection of trilobites. These three-lobed marine invertebrates dominated the world's oceans for many millions of years, and their fossils are abundant in Paleozoic rocks and clays. Trilobites were long gone by the time dinosaurs appeared about 225 million years ago. Even trilobites are difficult to find on the college Web site, but talented surfers may succeed in locating information on them. Try the Geology Department home page.

ADDRESS AND PHONE NUMBER:
Rennie Geology Museum
Dickinson College
Carlise, PA 17013
(717) 245-1448

Rutgers University Geology Museum
www-rci.edu/~geolweb/museum.htm

Dinosaurs must have liked New Jersey, since they left their foot-prints all over the state. Mesozoic trackways are the highlight of the geology museum at Rutgers, the famed New Jersey state university. In addition to the trackways, the museum serves up a considerable variety of dinosaur fossils, including a skull cast of an *Allosaurus* and a mounted skeleton of a *Maiasaura*. There is also a mastodon, along with other prehistoric mammal remains. Much of the fossil material was found in New Jersey. The Web sites listed above may not be the only way to reach the Rutgers Geology Museum on-line, but try them first. Afterward, you can surf around a bit and see what you find.

ADDRESS AND PHONE NUMBER:

Rutgers University Geology Museum
College Avenue
New Brunswick, NJ 08903
(732) 932-7243

Santa Barbara Museum of Natural History
sbnature.org

You know you've hit on a super Web site here as soon as the home page illustration comes up on the screen. It's a magnificent painting of a long-necked sauropod fighting off a toothy predator. The Santa Barbara Museum of Natural History has done a great job on its site. Most of the sizzle, however, is found in marine displays, such as the enormous whale skeleton likely to dwarf the dinosaur models at some museums.

ADDRESS AND PHONE NUMBER:

Santa Barbara Museum of Natural History
2559 Puesta de Sol Road
Santa Barbara, CA 93105
(805) 682-4711

Schiele Museum of Natural History
www.schielemuseum.org

The Schiele Museum of Natural History is a fine place to learn about the development of life on the earth. Here fossils and dioramas trace the evolution of species over five hundred million years, from the development of the first single-cell life-forms to the appearance of far more complex creatures such as dinosaurs. The Web site provides a good overview of the museum. Go to the *Hall of Earth and Man* page for a photograph of the *T. rex* display.

ADDRESS AND PHONE NUMBER:
> Schiele Museum of Natural History
> 1500 East Garrison Boulevard
> Gastonia, NC 28056
> (704) 866-6908

Science Museum of Minnesota
www.smm.org/

Dino-hunters will find plenty to interest them at Saint Paul's noted Science Museum of Minnesota. In the Paleontology Hall they will encounter the world's largest mounted *Camptosaurus* skeleton, plus an eighty-foot-long *Diplodocus*, a menacing *Allosaurus*, and a *Tyrannosaurus* skull. Some of these exhibits can be sampled on-line at the Web site listed above.

ADDRESS AND PHONE NUMBER:
> Science Museum of Minnesota
> 120 West Kellogg Boulevard
> Saint Paul, MN 55102
> (651) 221-9444

Science Place

www.scienceplace.org/

The Science Place in Dallas and its site on the Web are mostly for kids—up to the age of about one hundred. There is a moving, roaring *T. rex* and the one on the *DinoDig* is fun, too—he wears sunglasses. Check out the museum's annual fundraising footrace called the Dinodash.

ADDRESS AND PHONE NUMBER:

The Science Place
P.O. Box 151469
Dallas, TX 75315
(214) 428-5555

South Carolina State Museum

www.museum.state.sc.us/

Wow! There are some really big jaws on display at the South Carolina State Museum in Columbia. You'll see them in the "Natural History" exhibit, and there is a photo on the museum home page. Otherwise, there's not much dinosaur stuff at this site. Even so, the museum is certainly worth a look, and you can get all the information you need for your visit at the Web site address above.

ADDRESS AND PHONE NUMBER:

South Carolina State Museum
301 Gervais Street
Columbia, SC 29201
(803) 898-4921

Springfield Science Museum
www.quadrangle.org/ssm.htm

You won't find much in the way of dinosaur stuff at this Web site, but you may want to visit the museum itself and enjoy its full-size models and mounted skeletons of *Tyrannosaurus rex, Stegosaurus,* and *Coelophysis* (a Late Triassic meat-eater). The site contains plenty of visitor information.

ADDRESS AND PHONE NUMBER:

Springfield Science Museum
220 State Street
Springfield, MA 01103
(413) 263-6800

Sternberg Memorial Museum of Natural History
www.fhsu.edu/sternberg/

The Sternberg Memorial Museum of Natural History in Hays, Kansas, contains one of the nation's largest and most spectacular paleontology exhibits. A Cretaceous diorama takes up nearly two whole floors of the museum. It offers a sweeping view of life on the planet some eighty million years ago and can be enjoyed by means of a walk-through tour. Unfortunately, the virtual tour accessible at the address above doesn't provide the full sweep of the experience. Nonetheless, you should pay this colorful and informative site a visit, as you'll see more dinosaurs here than on most other Internet museum tours.

ADDRESS AND PHONE NUMBER:

Sternberg Memorial Museum
3000 Sternberg Drive

Hays, KS 67601
(785) 628-4286

Texas Memorial Museum
www.utexas.edu/depts/tmm/

Fossils of the mighty flying reptile *Quetzalcoatlus* were discovered by a University of Texas student during a 1971 fossil-gathering expedition in the Big Bend region. Nowadays, the reconstructed fossil skeleton of *Quetzalcoatlus* flies over the Great Hall of the Texas Memorial Museum in Austin. You can get a good look at it by visiting the Web address listed above, but there is much more here of interest to the prehistory-minded Web surfer, including the famed Onion Creek mosasaur and Glen Rose trackways. You'll also find plenty of information about the museum's enormous collection of invertebrate fossils. The latter collection is the largest of its kind in the world, but the museum's dinosaur holdings are more limited. The museum displays several excellent mounted mosasaur skeletons, one of them in excess of thirty feet long and with a skull almost five feet long.

ADDRESS AND PHONE NUMBER:
Texas Memorial Museum
University of Texas
2400 Trinity Street
Austin, TX 78705
(512) 471-1604

University of Arkansas Museum
www.uark.edu/

The Web site allows you to check out the university and its science facilities. One of the excellent fossil exhibits at the university's small but rewarding campus museum features an early crocodile-like creature that lived and captured its prey in the vast swamps that covered Arkansas during much of the dinosaur era. Interestingly, crocodiles still inhabit the planet, while the dinosaurs—except for birds—have vanished. You won't find many dinosaurs at the university Web site either.

ADDRESS AND PHONE NUMBER:
University of Arkansas
202 Museum
Garland Street
Fayetteville, AR 72701
(501) 575-3555

University of Colorado Museum
www.colorado.edu/CUMUSEUM/

The University of Colorado is located right in the heart of dinosaur country and the fossil-rich Rocky Mountain region. Not surprisingly, the university's museum places special emphasis on its paleontology collections and exhibits. On display at the university's museum in Boulder are skulls of several large dinosaurs, including *Diplodocus* and *Triceratops*, along with many other major fossils. Little of this can be seen on the museum Web site, but you do get a good overview of what the museum has to offer.

ADDRESS AND PHONE NUMBER:
University of Colorado
Campus Box 218
Boulder, CO 80309
(303) 492-6892

University of Kansas Museum of Natural History
www.nhm.ukans.edu/

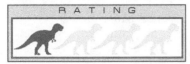

Useful if you happen to be planning a visit to the museum, this site has little in the way of dinosaur models, fossils, or information. In fact, there's not much here but a brief description of what you'll find in the museum. However, that should be enough to entice a visit from dino-lovers who'll want to see the museum's *Archaeopteryx* (an early birdlike dinosaur) and mounted *Pteranodon,* a flying reptile with an airplane-size wingspan of twenty-five feet. There are also remains of large marine reptiles, such as plesiosaurs and mosasaurs, and a massive *Triceratops* skull on display.

ADDRESS AND PHONE NUMBER:
University of Kansas Museum of Natural History
University of Kansas
Dyche Hall
Lawrence, KS 66045
(913) 864-4450

University of Michigan Exhibit Museum Paleontology Museum
www.exhibits.lsa.umich.edu/

You'll find a couple of excellent on-line paleontology exhibits here. One tells all about the *Deinonychus antirrhopus,* a relatively small but ferocious meat-eater, while the second takes you on a mastodon safari. Other fine on-line science exhibits at this site explore aspects of astronomy, anthropology, zoology, and much more. There is also plenty of information on the huge fossil collection at the University of Michigan Exhibit Museum. It contains more than two hundred thousand cataloged vertebrate specimens and nearly two million invertebrate specimens.

ADDRESS AND PHONE NUMBER:
University of Michigan Exhibit Museum
1109 Geddes Avenue
Ann Arbor, MI 48109
(313) 764-0478

University of Wisconsin Geology Museum
www.geology.wisc.edu/~museum/

You can download images of dozens of fossils at this site maintained by the University of Wisconsin Geology Museum. Some of these, such as the thirty-three-foot mounted skeleton of a duck-billed *Edmontosaurus* and sizable *Triceratops*-like *Avaceratops* are quite impressive. There are many mammal fossils, as well. Each display is accompanied by a brief but highly informative description.

ADDRESS AND PHONE NUMBER:
University of Wisconsin Geology Museum
1215 West Dayton Street
Madison, WI 53706
(608) 262-2399

University of Wyoming Geological Museum
www.uwyo.edu/geomuseum/

You'll see the head of a roaring *Allosaurus* on the home page at this address. Apparently, this is "Big Al," who serves as something of a mascot for the Geological Museum at the University of Wyoming. For a look at Big Al's twenty-five-foot-long mounted skeleton, take the virtual museum tour. Accompanying Big Al is a seventy-five-foot-long *Apatosaurus,* which probably weighed in at about twenty-five tons when it was alive during the Jurassic Period, as well as a soaring Late Cretaceous *Pteranodon,* a seven-foot-long *Triceratops* skull, and a huge *Tyrannosaurus* skull with bared teeth.

If you'd like to dig some dinosaurs yourself, click on the *Summer Field Program* option. There you'll find information on the museum's field expeditions. Open to amateur dinosaur enthusiasts, they allow you to dig for fossils right alongside expert paleontologists.

ADDRESS AND PHONE NUMBER:

University of Wyoming Geological Museum
P.O. Box 3006
Laramie, WY 82071
(307) 766-2646

Utah Prehistoric Adventures
www.utah.com

Maintained by the Utah Travel Council to attract visitors to their spectacular state, the site is a grab bag of colorful photography and travel information. Surf around and you'll eventually hit on the *Prehistoric Adventures* option—listed under *History/Heritage.* Here you'll find a wealth of material related to some of the world's most interesting dinosaur parks and museums. Some of these are not widely known but have much to offer the serious student of paleontology. Among the highlights are: the Eccles Dinosaur Park, where you can see more than sixty life-size dinosaur models; the Utah Field House, with its walk through time; the Dinosaur Garden, with its delightful sculpture; the College of Eastern Utah, with its mounted skeletons and dinosaur eggs; the Mile Canyon Dinosaur Trail near Moab; the Potash Road Dinosaur Tracks; the

Dinosaur Museum of Blanding, with its skeletons, paintings, and fossil displays; and much more.

ADDRESS AND PHONE NUMBER:
Utah Travel Council
P.O. Box 147420
Salt Lake City, UT 84114
(801) 538-1030

Virginia Museum of Natural History
www.vmnh.org/

The Virginia Museum of Natural History is alive with dinosaurs as well as prehistoric bugs. You'll see some of both at the above address. It offers a Dinosaur Gallery, featuring *Allosaurus, Apatosaurus, Euoplocephalus,* and *Parasaurolophus.* There are also some interesting field trips organized by the museum. A dinosaur digging expedition was offered during the summer of 1999.

ADDRESS AND PHONE NUMBER:
Virginia Museum of Natural History
1001 Douglas Avenue
Martinsville, VA 24112
(540) 666-8600

Wistariahurst Museum
www.holyoke.org/mainpage.htm

Something of a dinosaur itself, Holyoke's wonderful old Wistaria-hurst mansion contains a fascinating museum but not much material of prehistoric interest. However, on the grounds outside the mansion are the footprints of dinosaurs that passed through this area many millions of years ago. Flagstones used to build a covered porch at the back of the building contain tracks more than one hundred million years old. The Web site tells the story of both the museum and its mysterious dinosaur tracks.

ADDRESS AND PHONE NUMBER:
    Wistariahurst Museum
    238 Cabot Street
    Holyoke, MA 01040
    (413) 542-2216

APPENDIX

KEEPING TRACK OF YOUR DINO-SCORE

Hunting for dinosaurs on the Internet can open up whole new worlds for both kids and adults. By exploring the earth's remote past, we gain a better understanding of our planet as it is today—and of ourselves. Discovery and knowledge are their own rewards, and we really don't need a yardstick to measure their value. Even so, some dino-hunters like to keep track of how well they are doing. After all, keeping count of things can be fun. So, here is a handy way to score your Internet dino-hunting progress:

1. Give yourself **one point** for each new dinosaur you encounter on the Internet. The dinosaur's Latin name—*Tyrannosaurus rex,* for instance—will do. Just list the name in your Internet Dinosaur Journal and give yourself a point, but only one point for each type of dinosaur, please.

2. Give yourself **two points** for locating photographic fossil evidence of your dinosaur. Many Web pages are illustrated with color pictures of fossils, and these are nearly always identified. When you find a clearly identified fossil photo, make note of it in your journal and give yourself two more points—but only once for each type of dinosaur.

    By doing this you will "virtually" retrace the steps of generations of hardworking natural historians. Keep in mind that fossils have always been the raw material of paleontology. Fossils—the mineralized bones of creatures that lived millions of years ago—are among the earth's foremost scientific treasures. With enough fossils in hand—sometimes only a few are necessary—scientists have made reasonably accurate assumptions about what dinosaurs looked like and how they lived.

3. Give yourself **three points** for searching out a Web page with a photograph showing a full mounted skeleton of the dinosaur you are researching. Articulated or reassembled skeletons show how paleontologists have pieced together their evidence and can reveal much about a long-extinct animal and how it lived. Be sure the dinosaur skeleton is properly identified. If you wish, you can substitute a panel depicting an artist's rendering or full-size model.

At this stage you may have scored up to six points for each dinosaur you've found on the Internet. But raising that score to ten points will take more work. To earn the four additional points you need, you'll have to track down a Web page or research paper posted on the Internet and dedicated exclusively to your dinosaur. That's not always easy, and in many cases will be impossible. But keep on looking and don't lose patience. The Internet is huge, and fresh material is added every day—especially on popular topics such as dinosaurs.

Here's a hint to get you started. Chicago's Field Museum— you can look up the address in chapter 7 (page 116)—has devoted an entire section of its Web site to "Sue," the famous *Tyrannosaurus rex* skeleton recently excavated in South Dakota. Visit the Field Museum address and you'll score a quick ten points for *T. rex.*

The scoring works the same for each dinosaur type. Let's say you've gone the full distance with *Allosaurus,* the fierce Jurassic meat-eater. Having noted the Latin name *Allosaurus* (one point), located a fossil photo (two points), searched out a full-size skeleton or model (three points), and found a research paper or dedicated Web page (four points), you've tallied the maximum score of ten points for this particular animal. Since paleontologists have identified many different types of dinosaurs, and most can be found somewhere on the World Wide Web, you can run your Internet dinosaur score into the thousands. All it takes is patience and a little hard work. And just think how much you'll learn.

NOTE: This scoring system was devised especially for use on the Internet. It's different from the one described in *Dino Safari,* but there's no need to get them confused. Just keep two different score sheets or files in your Dino-Journal.

KEEPING AN ON-LINE DINOSAUR JOURNAL

You'll learn more and have more fun if you keep a journal of your Internet dinosaur adventures. You may want to dedicate a hard-disk file for this purpose, since you'll likely want to save a very large volume of material. That way it will be easy to download entire files and photographs of your favorite dinosaurs.

You might include fossils, skeletons, and models you've seen, personal observations and insights, or even entire printed Web pages. Subfiles might be dedicated to particular lines of inquiry, such as the link between modern birds and dinosaurs, or to controversies such as the one that still rages over dinosaur extinction.

Your journal will help you organize your dinosaur research. If you are a student, it could become the basis of an award-winning science project. Otherwise, it will serve as a fine way to get more enjoyment out of your hobby and to share it with others. After all, friends and family can't always be at your side when you're surfing the Net.

INDEX OF LISTINGS

INDEX OF RATINGS